Withdrawn

Creative Thinking and Brainstorming

For P with love

Creative Thinking and Brainstorming

J GEOFFREY RAWLINSON

Gower

First published in hardback in 1981 by
Gower Publishing Company Limited

Paperback edition first published 1983 by
Gower Publishing Company
Gower House
Croft Road
Aldershot
Hants GU11 3HR
England

Gower
Old Post Road
Brookfield
Vermont 05036
USA

Reprinted 1986, 1988, 1989, 1993, 1994

© J. Geoffrey Rawlinson

British Library Cataloguing in Publication Data

Rawlinson, J. G.
   Creative thinking and brainstorming
   1. Problem solving   2. Management   3. Creative ability
   I. Title
   658.4′03   HD30.29

ISBN 0 7045 0543 6

Printed and bound in Great Britain by
Biddles Limited, Guildford and King's Lynn

CONTENTS

PREFACE

This book is addressed to any manager at any level in an organisation, an enterprise, or a group of people working together to find solutions to problems. It seeks to satisfy two long-felt and unsatisfied needs in the field of creativity:

1 a simple account of the best and most widely used creativity technique — brainstorming. This account should include a step-by-step methodology and a look at the associated techniques of restating the problem and the wildest idea, and should set out procedures for the evaluation of the large number of ideas obtained in the brainstorming session.

2 a view of creative thinking in relation to brainstorming and the other techniques used in this field. This includes the identification of the barriers which prevent managers from successfully using their innate creative ability.

While there are some books which touch on both these needs, none gives a clear enough picture to enable managers to introduce brainstorming in their organisations; and none of them deals adequately with the preliminary stages of identifying the barriers to creative thinking.

The material in the present book has been generated from a series of presentations on creative thinking and brainstorming which I gave during the years 1966-79. These presentations took place in the United Kingdom, some European countries, Venezuela and the Caribbean, Nigeria, Malaysia, Singapore and Hong Kong.

Over seventy one-day seminars were run for the British Institute of Management, and some hundreds for other organisations and companies, together with half-day creative thinking and brainstorming introductions on training courses at Sundridge Park Management Centre and elsewhere. The ability to use brainstorming in solving client's problems is included in the armoury of my consultant colleagues in PA International Management Consultants Limited. Many successful brainstorming sessions have been run with clients and within PA on a wide range of topics.

All these have contributed considerable experience and knowhow. This book seeks to pass on this experience, in the hope that brainstorming will be used more successfully in organisations to find solutions to difficult problems.

It is hardly necessary to state that the objective of problem solving is to find solutions to an organisation's problems. There are many routes that can be followed and brainstorming is just one of these routes. Clearly none of them can be guaranteed to lead to solutions — and brainstorming is no exception to this rule. While a brainstorming session *will* give a large number of ideas, it only *may* give solutions. In addition, it is the solution which is implemented that matters, not the route used to reach it. This is a totally correct perspective, and it does not, or should not, matter in the very least that brainstorming or any of the other techniques was the route followed. One difference, however, can be demonstrated in brainstorming as a problem-solving technique. The actual brainstorming session itself is fun, generating a good deal of laughter, enjoyment and a sense of taking part in solving the problems of management — and why shouldn't there be laughter? As one eminent management writer says, 'If you're not in business to have fun, what the hell are you doing here?' (with acknowledgement to Robert Townsend).

An essential first step in the introduction of brainstorming is for managers to be made aware of, and to lower, a number of barriers to creative thinking. These barriers are inculcated in all of us at a very early age. One has only to compare the more serious approach to games and, indeed, learning as the child enters his or her teens, with the highly creative and enjoyable games of very young children. This process is continued through school, university, professional and technical training so that managers tend to have a well-developed analytical ability, and a poorly developed creative ability. This creative ability is further stultified by the barriers, and a sense that management is a serious business, rarely to be enjoyed and laughed about. This explains why the second of the needs mentioned above is considered first in the sequence of chapters in the book.

Chapter 1 — on creative thinking — distinguishes between analytical thinking and creative thinking, and identifies the most important of the barriers preventing managers from being creative. An awareness of the contents of this chapter alone will ensure improvement in the conduct of meetings between two or more managers in any organisation.

Chapters 2 and 3 look at brainstorming, define it and discuss the running of brainstorming sessions. The objective in these chapters is to highlight the 'tricks of the trade' in the running of brainstorming sessions, so that the reader will feel confident enough to try the technique in his own organisation. The importance of restating the problem, and the benefits of the wildest idea technique, are described. Chapter 3 ends with a checklist of dos and don'ts in brainstorming.

Chapter 4 looks at evaluation. The well-run brainstorming session will produce hundreds of ideas. Many of them, in the cold light of next day, may appear to be silly, rubbishy or totally inappropriate. A systematic procedure is required to avoid discarding all the ideas — and 'throwing the baby out with the bath water'. A brainstorming session which produces one winner of an idea is time very well spent. But one winner in a pile of, say, four hundred discarded ideas gives a measure of task of evaluation and makes apparent the size of the haystack in which the needle of a good idea is buried. The chapter identifies a number of mechanisms which can be used.

Chapter 5 suggests ways of introducing brainstorming in organisations whose members have not taken part in brainstorming sessions before. As with most techniques, there is a right and a wrong way. Failure to introduce brainstorming carefully not only destroys any hope of solving the particular problem; it also kills the concept of brainstorming for many years in the organisation. 'Brainstorming', people will say, 'just another gimmick which produces only a few ideas and a large amount of rubbish!' Procedures to be followed for the first introduction of brainstorming, and for subsequent brainstorming sessions, are suggested.

Chapter 6 gives some examples from my experience in running and evaluating brainstorming sessions. Chapter 7 looks briefly at some other techniques for developing creativity. While none of these has such wide application as brainstorming, they have been applied in a variety of fields and produced some useful ideas. There is a bibliography listing some of the books in the field of creative thinking and brainstorming, and a glossary of terms.

I believe that in any organisation and at any level in that organisation, there exists a deep untapped well of useful ideas. Creative thinking seeks to tap this well for the greater benefit of the organisation and the people in general. It does require considerable effort, not only to introduce creativity techniques in face of scepticism and disbelief, but also in the follow-up of a brainstorming session in evaluation and implementation. Creative thinking and the creativity techniques can be taught — in particular, managers can be weaned away from their well-tried analytical techniques and prejudices, into the rewarding and enjoyable fields of brainstorming. It is this belief that runs like a thread through the whole of this book.

Newbiggin   J. Geoffrey Rawlinson
Cumbria   November 1980

ACKNOWLEDGEMENTS

Pride of place goes to Brian P. Smith, sometime director of research and development, and later chief executive of PA Management Consultants Ltd, now Wolfson professor of design management at the Royal College of Art in London. BPS led me into the creative road, and provided much encouragement.

Many other colleagues in PA International Management Consultants Ltd have helped in creative sessions, or in running brainstorming talks. Especial thanks go to Alan Popham and David Hawley.

My thanks, too, to the many managers and organisations in the United Kingdom and overseas who have listened to my seminars, and who have provided so many practical examples. Notable among these organisations is the British Institute of Management, for whom I have run so many one-day seminars.

Chapter 7 discusses other techniques in the creative field. Two of these are synectics and PO. Synectics originated in the USA, and is pioneered in the UK by Abraxas Management Research. My thanks are due to Vincent Nolan and his colleagues who allowed me to attend one of their courses on synectics. PO is the brainchild of Dr Edward de Bono, and is described in his books on lateral thinking — my thanks to him.

Many books listed in the bibliography have provided guidance and inspiration. In particular, Alex Osborn's 'Applied Imagination' and Arthur Koestler's 'Act of Creation' are gratefully acknowledged. The puzzle books of Martin Gardner and H.E. Dudeney provided much fun of both analytical and creative types. 'You and Creativity' by Kaiser Aluminum provided good background material. Finally, the monthly publication of Sidney X. Shore, 'Creativity in Action', and Sidney's letters and visits to the UK, are always full of creative ideas. My thanks to these and others not mentioned.

Finally, my thanks to secretaries in PA and at Sundridge Park who have typed the ideas (some unprintable!) recorded on newsprint in brainstorming sessions. In particular, Linda Magrath who has also typed and retyped successive drafts of this book.

J.G.R.

1 Creative thinking

One of the prerequisites for the application of creativity techniques is an awareness of the barriers which hinder creativity, and their removal. This chapter first defines creative thinking, distinguishing it from analytical thinking, and goes on to identify the major barriers which hinder creativity.

Without exception, everybody has creative ability. One only has to watch, unobserved, the games which young children play on their own or in groups, to see how strongly this ability is present. Unfortunately, as children grow up they are conditioned to submerge this creative ability within other abilities. Life at school in the educational routines that they have to follow, and subsequent education in university, technical, professional or practical fields develop the other abilities strongly at the expense of the innate creative ability. In fact, it goes further — in many cases the creative approach to tackling problems is actively discouraged.

There is a story of a university student sitting a physics examination. One question asked, 'Given a barometer, how would you tell the height of a tall building?'. The student answered as follows: 'I would take the barometer to the roof, lower it on a piece of string to the ground. I would then haul it up again, and measure the length of the string'. The examiner was not pleased and awarded the student no marks. On disputing this award, the student asked for an independant arbitrator to adjudicate. The arbitrator, hearing both sides, offered the student another chance at the same question. The student accepted, and wrote his answer: 'I would measure the barometric pressure at ground level and on the roof. The difference can be converted into the height of the building'. The examiner, sensing defeat, accepted the answer, and awarded 98 percent. The arbitrator later asked the student why he had tried to make a fool of the examiner. The student first gave some further answers — why not try it for yourself before looking at the end of this chapter? — and then said: 'I am fed up with your physics course inhibiting my creativity. I wanted to demonstrate that there were other, equally valid, answers to the question'. (NB Other answers to the barometer question, and to the puzzles appearing later are given at the end of the chapter.)

In other words, the educational system unwittingly raises barriers, which prevent men and women from being creative. It is these barriers which must be identified and removed. Further, in the creative situation, such as a brainstorming session, these barriers must be lowered, for they have no part to play in the free-wheeling atmosphere engendered. On several occasions, I have arranged for a hat stand to be placed outside the room in which the brainstorming session is to be held. When the participants arrived, they were asked to go outside the room and hang their barriers on the hat stand!

Analytical and creative thinking

Consider this problem:

> A Scotsman was celebrating his golden wedding anniversary with a family reunion. He had arranged a dinner party in a private room in a local hotel with a piper to welcome his guests on the bagpipes. Shortly after the party started, he looked around the family and noticed that there were present:
>
> | | |
> |---|---|
> | 1 grandfather | 2 sisters |
> | 1 grandmother | 2 sons |
> | 2 fathers | 2 daughters |
> | 2 mothers | 1 father-in-law |
> | 4 children | 1 mother-in-law |
> | 3 grandchildren | 1 daughter-in-law |
> | 1 brother | |
>
> Being a canny Scotsman, he had budgeted carefully, and had the exact money to pay for the party in his sporran. Assuming that the piper was included in the cost of £10 per head, how much money did the Scotsman have in his sporran?

A swift glance at the list of guests and adding up the numbers would lead to a figure of £230. Not believing that the Scotsman would be so rash as to spend £230 on a dinner for his relatives, a second and possibly more suspicious look at the family leads to the realisation that some members of the party may have dual roles, i.e. as a father and a son. This leads to a reconsideration of the family and saves the Scotsman a considerable amount of cash.

Apart from a slight feeling of being led up the garden path, or being fooled, the solution to this problem requires logical thinking or counting, and it leads to a unique answer. Because logical thinking or counting is involved, let us define this problem as an analytical problem. (A comment on the size of the Scotsman's family is made at the end of this chapter).

Consider now another problem: Suppose you were invited to join a government department on secondment from your organisation. You find that the team of civil servants and yourself are considering the problem — 'How to persuade families to take their holidays in Britain this year?' This is a different sort of problem from the Scotsman's family. Not just one answer, there are many possible ways of persuading people to take their holidays in Britain. It does, however, need a certain amount of imagination to overcome the image of mackintoshes and wet walks, particularly when confronted with glossy brochures showing seaside places in the Mediterranean. As imagination is involved, let us define this as a creative problem.

We identified two sorts of problems — analytical and creative — and logically enough, two sorts of thinking are required. These are shown in the Figure 1.1, together with four of the technical terms associated with analytical and creative thinking.

Analytical thinking is logical and leads to unique or few answers, which can be implemented. Creative thinking requires imagination, and leads to many possible answers or ideas. While the two sorts of thinking are different, they are linked because one sort complements the other. This is evident in creative thinking, where the many ideas must later be analysed to sort out the few that can be implemented. Analytical thinking consolidates ideas and practices, and must be followed by creative leaps if progress is to be made.

Figure 1.1 contains four of the technical terms, or

ANALYTICAL	CREATIVE
Logic	Imagination
Unique (or few) answers	Many possible answers or ideas
CONVERGENT	DIVERGENT
VERTICAL	LATERAL

Figure 1.1   Two sorts of thinking

'buzzwords', which are common in the vocabulary of management. These are 'convergent, divergent, vertical and lateral'. In contrast to most buzzwords, these four are simple, straightforward words which convey easily understood meanings.

Analytical thinking is convergent, narrowing down to unique answers or a small number of ideas which can be further analysed and implemented. Creative thinking is divergent, starting from the description of the problem and diverging to give many ideas for solving it, or possible answers to it. In effect, analytical thinking produces solutions and creative thinking produces ideas — large numbers of them from which the solution can be selected. Convergent and divergent are appearing more frequently in the literature of creative thinking and in the articles in management papers. The two words are more colourful than analytical and creative and they do convey a mental picture of the process being followed.

The other two words — vertical and lateral — are less well-known but are equally applicable in the context of analytical and creative thinking. Tackling a problem in the analytical way requires deep, and possibly narrow, probing to identify all aspects — hence vertical thinking. On the other hand, creative thinking requires a wide-ranging examination of all the options, including those which might be considered to be wild or foolish, and those which appear to be outside and not linked at all with the problem — hence lateral thinking. Of the two words, lateral thinking is the commoner due to the work on creative thinking by Doctor Edward de Bono (see Bibliography on page 119).

The two sorts of thinking can be linked in another way.

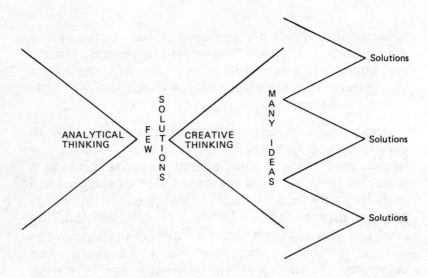

Figure 1.2 Two sorts of thinking

In Figure 1.2, convergent (analytical) and divergent (creative) thinking are illustrated with few solutions and many ideas. The process can be continued indefinitely, where creative thinking is again used on a solution to generate more ideas. The figure has two misleading features. The perspectives of analytical and creative suggest that people are better at creative thinking than analytical. As we shall see, the reverse is true. Secondly there is the deliberate separation of analytical and creative, and this is not representative of real life. Everybody has a creative ability. Unfortunately it is buried within analytical thinking, and this tends to kill the creative ideas too quickly. 'That's silly' we say, and the idea is discarded. Conscious and deliberate separation is required.

As a final example, imagine you have a piece of 5-ply board, which has three holes cut in it. The holes are triangular, circular and square in shape. You are asked to describe a solid wooden object which will go through each hole, right through and pull clear of the back. When the object is in any hole, it is a tight fit, i.e. the wooden surface touches the 5-ply board at all points of the hole.

At first thought, this seems an impossible object. It is easy to get two out of the three. For example a wooden cone satisfies the circle and triangle, and a pyramid satisfies the triangle and square, but all three seem quite impossible. One non-solution is a rod, machined circular at one end, triangular in the centre, and square at the other end. Unfortunately this object will not pass completely through the board.

The solution requires both creative and analytical thinking: creative in seeing the solid wooden object (in your mind's eye); analytical in being able to describe it simply in words. A drawing of the object appears at the end of this chapter. Looking at this, it is clear that the three views are obtained by turning the object so as to see it from three different directions at right angles to each other. 'A tent-shaped wedge on a circular base', is one description. An even simpler way to describe it is, 'Take a cylinder of wood and cut off a length equal to the diameter — there's the basis of the circle and square. Scribe a line across a diameter, and cut to this line from opposite edges to form a wedge'. Notice that the wedge must be tent-shaped, and that two cuts are required. One cut, from one corner to the opposite corner gives a wrong sort of triangle, and will not give the square at all.

This is an example of both creative and analytical thinking, working together. It is, of course, possible to arrive at the shape by analytical thinking only, as most engineers would confirm. In fact I have used this example in many seminars and talks, and am constantly amazed and disheartened by the small number of people who can describe the object. Most people say that it is impossible.

Definition of creative thinking

This chapter examines creative thinking and it is therefore appropriate to define what is meant by the term. Creative thinking is:

> The relating of things or ideas which were previously unrelated.

Humour, or the well-told joke, illustrates this definition completely. The punchline at the end of the joke takes the listener into a strange field, unrelated until the story teller makes a relationship (and the listener accepts it).

This relationship is totally apparent after it has been made, but the strangeness of the connection contributes to the other factors making for the success of the joke. Notice that creative thinking uses things or ideas which are already in existence, that is, in the minds of those taking part in the creative session. It does not seek to invent new concepts, although the final outcome may appear to be new through the joining of two or more existing concepts.

Another technical term used to describe creative thinking is 'bisociative thinking'. The word 'Bisociation' was coined by Arthur Koestler, and described in his book *The Act of Creation* (see Bibliography). Bisociative thinking imagines a manager tackling a problem moving around on a plane or matrix. He is kept on the surface of the plane by all the conventional rules and habits of analytical thinking and he does not find an acceptable solution. Koestler imagines a second plane or matrix cutting first. The manager meets the plane and moves into it to find a possible answer to the problem. The two planes are unrelated until the manager establishes the relationship, and finds the possible answer to the problem in the second plane. The establishment of the relationship, or bisociation, is usually accompanied by a release of tension — the 'Aha' reaction or the flash of illumination revealing an answer. This is exactly mirrored in the analogy of the joke, where the punchline establishes a new and previously unthought of relationship, resulting in laughter.

Many examples of bisociative thinking exist, particularly in the field of scientific discovery. The separate ideas of ocean tides and the movement of the moon must have been known for thousands of years. It was only in the seventeenth century that Keppler linked the two. A contemporary astronomer, Galileo, laughed at the idea as mere superstition. Another example is the invention of the printing press by Gutenburg. He went to a wine harvest, and in the celebration party saw the wine press as the solution to the problem of printing evenly from hundreds of individual seals or letters. The founder of organic chemistry, Professor August von Kekulé, was said to have dreamed of a snake biting its tail, and this lead to the ring structure of six carbon atoms in Benzene. William Harvey watched the heart of a living fish beating on the fishmonger's slab, and realised that it was merely a pump. Alexander Fleming waited fifteen years for the spores of penicillin notatum to blow through his laboratory window on to a dish of staphylococci. Years earlier he had noticed the killing of other baccilli in a culture dish with outside agents.

These examples of bisociation emphasise that the information must be there to be combined in different and new ways. The creative man spots the link and makes the discovery. As Louis Pasteur said: 'Fortune favours the prepared mind'. Bisociative thinking is a powerful concept in the field of creativity, and links closely with the definition of creative thinking given above.

An aspect of creative thinking is dreaming. Dreaming is believed to be an essential requirement in the way in which the brain works, and there are very few people who do not dream. Recall a dream — this may be difficult — and think analytically about it. The images appear to be quite unrelated, disturbingly so in some cases. They move from one scene to another, with effortless ease and no apparent links. The links must be there although considerable effort may be required to establish them. Dreaming, or day-dreaming as it is sometimes called, is not considered to be part of the analytical manager's kit of tools. In fact, it is actively discouraged. How often have you heard the phrase: 'I wouldn't dream of doing that'? I believe that dreaming should be a part of every manager's way of life. Perhaps if he allowed himself to dream a little bit more and established some of those curious relationships, the options available in problem solving would be wider and would lead to better solutions.

The barriers to creative thinking

It has already been established that there are two sorts of thinking — analytical and creative — and that the average manager is better at analytical thinking because of his background. While everybody has an innate creative ability, there seem to be barriers which prevent the average manager from using it effectively. It is these barriers which will now be discussed. The identification and acceptance of them, and their removal in creative sessions is an essential requirement.

As a first step in the identification of the barriers, take a piece of paper and imagine an ordinary paper-clip. In the next two minutes, jot down as many good uses as you can think of, and be prepared to read the list out to somebody — say your wife or a colleague or your secretary. Notice two points in the instructions: 'good uses' and 'read the list out'. Keep these two in mind while jotting down ideas.

After two minutes — which may appear to be a considerable length of time, particularly if only a few ideas have been identified — draw a line under the final idea and count up the total. The total may be anything between nil and fifteen or more, though in my experience, three to six are the more common figures. Put the list on one side, we will return to it a little later in the chapter.

There are a number of barriers which get in the way of the analytical managers. The more important are:

> self-imposed barriers;
> patterns, or one unique answer;
> conformity;
> not challenging the obvious;
> evaluating too quickly;
> fear of looking a fool.

These are discussed below.

Self-imposed barriers

The self-imposed barrier is one of the more difficult barriers to recognise. We put it up ourselves, either consciously or unconsciously — if the latter, an understanding colleague or friend is required to point out (tactfully) our error. Once recognised, it is however one of the easy ones to dispose of.

Consider the following sentence:

> Rapid righting with his uninjured hand saved the contents of the capsized canoe.

When read from the printed word, the sentence makes complete sense and there seems to be nothing strange about it. But ask a colleague to take a piece of paper and jot the sentence down as you read it to him. For a short while, the sentence does not make sense — he will have spelt the second word with a 'w' i.e. 'writing'. (Lest he accuses you of misleading him, take care to ask him to '*jot* the sentence down'; he will say you used the words, 'write the sentence' and therefore deliberately misled him). The point here is that word 'write' is a more common word than 'right' and in hearing the first few words, most people go for the more common word. This is an example of the self-imposed barrier — a barrier that we put up unconsciously.

Now consider another problem. What do you make of this?

$$1 + 1 = ?$$

The obvious answer is two and everybody gets this, although with some slight hesitation, due to the suspicion that there may be other answers. In fact, of course there are, because the answer '2' is the analytical answer. Look at the problem again and derive some more answers — see end of the chapter.

Other answers require creative thinking or a questioning approach to the meanings of the symbols in the problem. For example, why not take the two ones and put them together, making 11. Or put one on top of the other and make a T. These are perfectly acceptable in the context of the question which said: 'What do you make of this?' The analytical man imposes his own rules — in this case an arithmetical one — which leads him inexorably to the one unique answer, '2'. But if the answer is not arithmetical, then there are two other symbols that can be used, + and =. There is no reason why these should not be used and lead to a considerable number of possible solutions.

The demonstration of the way in which the self-imposed barrier can be established is given by the following pair of examples. Arrange six dots in the shape of a triangle. Join all six dots with three straight lines without taking your pencil off the paper.

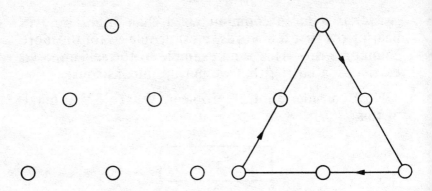

Notice how simple and straightforward it is. Now consider nine dots arranged in a square. This time join all nine dots using four straight lines without taking the pencil off the paper (retracing a line counts as two).

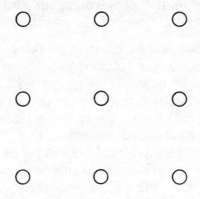

This is nothing like so simple a problem, in fact, you may require five lines to get to the centre dot. But notice the pre-conditioning from the six dots arranged in a triangle. The first attempt goes round the outside dots and requires a fifth line to reach the centre dot. The barrier here — dots in a square — is self-imposed. The solution requires the lines to go outside the square formed by the dots and this is difficult to accept, particularly with the pre-conditioning of the six dots. The solution is given at the end of the chapter. And as a final comment on the self-imposed barrier, try and join the nine dots with three straight lines without taking the pencil off the paper!

In presenting this problem in seminars, I find three states of mind in those attempting the problem. Firstly, the answer is known, is drawn in quickly, albeit with some complacency. Secondly, the problem has not been seen before, and the participants struggle with it for some time. Lastly, and possibly the worst state of all, some participants have seen the problem before, and cannot recall the answer!

Establishing a pattern or one unique answer

Another barrier is that the analytical man seeks to establish a pattern, or to find the one right answer. Having established the pattern, he may not be adventurous and establish other patterns that may equally well exist.

As an example, consider the relationship of the following letters

$$\frac{A \qquad E}{B \quad C \quad D}$$

The analytical man looking at the pattern knows immediately where to put *F*. But does he get *both* patterns, because *F* may go on top of the line or below the line, depending on the rules? For example, if the pattern established is vowels and consonants, *F* must go below the line. This is the more common pattern but there is another, equally valid pattern, depending on straight lines and curves. The letters *A* and *E* are made of straight lines, while the letters *B*, *C* and *D* contain curves. As *F* has only straight lines, *F* must go on top. The two patterns are complete and clear, and there is no doubt as to where *F* goes. There are other patterns, but these are mostly incomplete, and require later letters to give the complete picture. For example, the pattern may be 1 on top, 3 down below, in which case *F* must go down below. But this pattern is not as complete as the earlier two. Another, less complete, pattern could be envisaged as 1 on top, 3 below, 2 on top, 3 below etc., in which case *F* goes on top! But this is even more uncertain.

Having established a pattern, whether complete or uncertain, the analytical man sticks with it, and may not bother to look for other patterns. The creative man, on the other hand, may deliberately seek other patterns, or is happy to accept a number of patterns or even none at all.

This barrier — establishing a pattern or one unique answer — is a difficult one for the analytical man to lower. He is trained to seek an answer to a problem, and may be reluctant to try other possible answers when he has found one which works.

Conformity, or giving the answer expected

The barrier of conformity follows the previous barrier in the sense that many managers feel they have to conform to the patterns established by their colleagues in the organisation in which they work.

As an example, consider the diagram opposite: how many squares do you see?

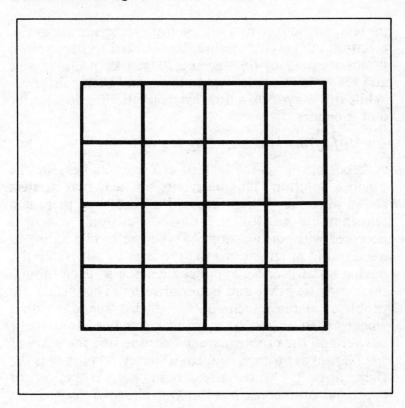

A quick count of the squares gives the answer 16. By this time however, you may be a little suspicious and look again at the pattern. You then notice that the squares themselves form a square, making 17. In addition, the squares are set in a frame which itself is also a square, making 18. There are in fact, many more squares than this — it is possible to identify over 200! The count is given in the notes at the end of the chapter.

The barrier illustrated by the squares is conformity. The manager has a need to conform to the pattern he believes his colleagues see or expect to see. An extreme example of conformity is the meeting attended by a relatively junior manager. In looking round those present, he notices that all the top executives are at the meeting. He may, therefore, be tempted to say 'I am a junior member of this meeting, I will keep quiet, wait and see which way the wind blows, and then conform'. While this may seem a little extreme, there is little doubt that it occurs.

Lack of effort in challenging the obvious

Another barrier is the lack of effort in challenging the obvious solution. This barrier is, in fact, two barriers rolled into one. When faced with problems, there is a tendency to go for the obvious answer, which is accepted without question. Maybe, we're just happy to have found an answer to the problem at all! Secondly, having an answer we avoid challenging it, even though there may be other and better answers. There is an old problem-solving technique which suggests that whenever an answer to a problem has been found, the answer and the problem are put on one side for a day or so. The answer is then challenged to test whether it is the right answer. More often than not, a period of conscious or unconscious thinking allows other answers to be found. These may be better, or at least may cast doubts on the original solution.

In general, managers tend to avoid following through ideas and suggestions which depart from the accepted state of affairs. The phrase, 'Why don't we ...?' is frequently answered in a negative way by working out the reasons why it cannot be done, or it would not work. For example, when we have to undertake a task which we do not very much like doing, we tend to 'put off the evil day', giving reasons why it would be better or more appropriate to tackle it at another time. If only we would buckle down and do it, the job would be completed in far less time than the time we spend finding excuses for not doing it!

An extreme statement of this barrier — lack of effort in challenging the obvious — is a response known as the 'automatic no'. Any new idea is automatically rejected, almost without consideration. The reason for the rejection may be that the new idea came from a junior, a peer or even someone outside the department or section. The rejector has feelings of anger or jealousy at not thinking of the idea himself, and therefore rejects it out of hand.

A phrase that illustrates this barrier is, 'you can't make a silk purse out of a sow's ear'. This is an impressive phrase and is used to justify taking no action. It was much used by the rather old-fashioned director of a chemistry laboratory. He tried to discourage the wilder ideas of the young members of staff by saying to them: 'Go away and think again, you can never make a silk purse out of a sow's ear'. Two of the younger members were so fed up with this admonition that they said: 'Come on, let's try'. They went down to the local slaughterhouse and bought a hundred pairs of sows' ears. These were genuine sows' ears, only sold by the pair, and the young men were given a certificate of origin. Taking them back to the laboratory, they treated them chemically and extracted a silk filament which their mothers knitted into a silk purse. They were delighted, and the director not a little aggrieved, when the silk purse was put on display on the laboratory noticeboard.

Evaluating too quickly

This barrier — evaluating too quickly — is not an easy one to remove. Everybody has a well developed capability of evaluating ideas, and this is applied almost instinctively when ideas are put forward. As with the 'automatic no' response, we tend to analyse and all too often reject ideas which are slightly offbeat or new:

'That's silly', 'That won't work' or 'We tried it last year and it didn't work then' are common phrases. The idea is then buried and a chance has been lost to develop new approaches.

One way of understanding this barrier is to look at your hands. If the left hand represents idea production and the right hand represents idea evaluation, the two hands are not separate as in real life but are linked and linked very tightly indeed. So much so, that an idea produced is immediately evaluated and possibly killed, e.g. by the phrase, 'that won't work'.

Success in creative thinking demands that the two linked hands should be separated, and that the right hand (idea evaluation) should be put on one side, for the moment. All ideas are acceptable in a creative situation, regardless of their quality. They may be good, bad, useful, useless, illegal — it doesn't matter, for in a creative session all ideas are acceptable. Subsequently, the evaluation hand is brought back and at that stage a strange thing happens. Some of the ideas, which would have originally been dismissed out of hand, are looked at afresh, possibly with the comment: 'Wait a minute, there may be something in that idea after all'. The ideas are given a chance to develop and not rejected too quickly. While the original idea may be silly or useless, it may lead onto other ideas which are readily applicable. So evaluation has no part to play in a creative situation, and all ideas, however wild or silly are accepted. Later, at the end of the session one or two really wild ideas are examined afresh — this is the basis of the wildest idea technique, a part of brainstorming which is described in Chapter 2.

Linked to this barrier, is the phrase, 'suspend judgement'. In the creative situation no evaluation or judgement is allowed, either of other people's ideas or

your own. Judgement is suspended until later and all
ideas are accepted.

Fear of looking a fool

Fear of looking a fool is the biggest barrier of all and the
most difficult to remove. It is one of the oldest barriers
in that it starts very early in life. The imagination and
creativity injected into games played by very young
children generate much laughter and enjoyment.
Unfortunately, the laughter can be turned against an
individual who then begins to say, 'they are laughing at
me'. Nobody likes being laughed at and, as a
consequence, as we grow up we tend to avoid putting
forward the silly or wild ideas, in case we are laughed at,
or thought foolish. Another phrase applicable in the
creative situation is 'laugh *with*, not *at*, the wild ideas'.

This barrier is heightened when managers from
different levels in the organisation are working together
to solve problems. The most junior member of the team
will not put forward wild ideas in case his seniors regard
him as a fool. He does not want to destroy his
promotion chances and therefore, sticks with well-tried
(i.e. analytical) routines. At the other end of the scale,
the most senior manager seeks to protect the image he
has built for himself. He says, 'I don't want to confirm
junior in his opinion that I'm a silly old fool'. As a
consequence, he does not propose any wild ideas either.

This barrier has another aspect. Managers do not like
going against universally accepted views, particularly
when these are stated by prominent or notable people.
There is a risk of being wrong, particularly if the new
idea is radically different from common practice.
Examples of this aspect abound in history, and are still
found today. This aspect is also particularly strong
when technological advance is present, and new skills

are required to replace existing. Examples of this aspect are:

> a castiron plough, invented in 1797, was rejected by New Jersey farmers who said that it would stimulate the weeds and poison the plants;
>
> the patent for a radio valve lapsed in 1907 as no-one could find a use for it;
>
> in 1906, a scientist, Simon Newcombe, said that flying was quite impossible;
>
> President Truman was said to have been advised by Admiral Leahy that, 'Atomic bombs won't go off, and I speak as an explosives expert';
>
> the railway builders in the early nineteenth century were advised that speeds of 50 m.p.h. would cause nose bleeds, and that trains could not go through tunnels because people would be asphyxiated;
>
> Brunel, building the SS 'Great Britain', now restored in dry dock in Bristol, was advised that, 'iron ships won't float'. So unsure were the builders of the efficiency of boilers and propellers that they included sails as well;
>
> in 1933, Lord Rutherford said, 'The energy produced by breaking down the atom is a poor kind of a thing. Anyone who expects a source of power from transformation of these atoms is talking moonshine';
>
> in 1957, the Astronomer Royal, Sir Harold Spencer Jones, commenting on the news of the first satellite, said that generations would pass before man landed on the moon, and that even if he did succeed, he would have precious little chance of getting back.

Statements like these made by eminent people, who really ought to know better, discourage others from trying new and unusual ideas. Fortunately creative people are prepared to take risks — it is they who lead the way into new technologies and procedures. They are not discouraged by criticism and, of course, are rightly acclaimed later when their ideas are found to be sound and workable.

Fear of looking foolish, or being proved wrong, is a powerful barrier for the analytical manager. As has been suggested earlier, barriers have no place in a creative session, and should be left outside the room.

Summary of the barriers

Summarising the barriers, we have identified self-imposed barriers; establishing a pattern or one unique answer; conformity or giving the answer expected; lack of effort in challenging the obvious; evaluating too quickly; and fear of looking a fool. In a creative situation, these barriers must be lowered or removed, and a free-wheeling atmosphere generated in which all ideas are acceptable no matter how silly or wild.

Remember the paper-clip — go back to your list and see how many more you can add to the list. Use 'suspend judgement', and write down all the ideas you can think of, including wild or silly ideas. A list (not exhaustive) is given in the solutions to problems at the end of the chapter.

Stages of thinking

There are five main stages in the thinking process and all need to be practised consciously, to get the best results from a creative thinking session. The stages are preparation; effort; incubation; insight (aha!); and evaluation.

These stages are described in turn and all of them are used in the brainstorming technique described in the next chapter.

Preparation

This is the first stage and consists in obtaining as many of the facts as possible about the problem. Of course, it is never possible to have all the facts, but a conscious and deliberate effort is required to obtain enough information. Care is necessary however, for too much information may inhibit creativity, by providing reasons why a new idea will not work. In particular, when establishing a team for a brainstorming session, outsiders to the problem are essential. They do not know that an idea will not work, or has been tried and found useless, and will suggest it. An example of this is given in the next chapter on brainstorming — in the section, 'State the problem and discuss'.

An important step in the preparation stage is the technique of restating the problem. While this is the second stage in running a brainstorming session, it is, however, a powerful mechanism for problem solving in its own right. Most of the problems managers have are not just like a football held in the hand, with the manager looking at it and saying, 'What am I going to do about this?' They are more like those large beach balls, two metres in diameter, blocking our view and preventing forward movement on the problem. Restating the problem suggests stepping back from it, walking round it, climbing over the top of it and peering inside. Facets of sectors of the beach ball (problem) are identified and written down. A manager may have only one view of the problem — restating it is a simple way of finding other views. It also provides the way out for the obstinate manager who resents a colleague's remark, 'For heaven's sake, that's not your real problem. Your real problem is ...'. The different view of the problem may well be the right one, but the manager is reluctant to accept it. Restating the problem is the means whereby other views of it can be given by other people, and accepted by the manager.

If you have a problem — most of us have! — try restating it in as many ways as possible, in particular remembering the guideline of suspend judgement described above. Take a large sheet of paper and write the problem on top. Ask some friends, colleagues, secretary to join you and to help you to restate the problem and write down their ideas. Use the mechanism, 'How to ...' described in the next chapter on brainstorming. You will be surprised at the number of restatements or different ways of looking at the problem, and you may get pointers to useful solutions.

Effort

Considerable effort is required in the second stage, together with divergent or creative thinking. This can lead to a certain amount of frustration, typified by the example of having to introduce a friend to a third person and not being able to remember the friend's name. We are embarrassed at being put on the spot, for we do not like to ask him in case he resents it, or thinks we are being rude. As a result we fail to introduce him properly and cause even more embarrassment!

A phrase which enshrines this frustration is, 'It's on the tip of my tongue'. We just cannot reach the idea, and considerable effort may be required to release it. Alternatively if we do, or think of, something else, the idea may be released spontaneously, as in incubation (discussed below).

This sort of frustration appears in a creative session and there are ways of overcoming it. Getting through the frustration is not easy, but it is usually found that very productive ideas are obtained shortly afterwards.

Incubation

Incubation is the third stage in the thinking process. This consists of allowing the problem to lie fallow in our minds while we do other tasks or tackle other problems. A typical phrase is, 'We're not going to solve this problem tonight, let's go home and sleep on it'. We do just this and in the morning we find that other possible solutions have appeared. It seems as if the mind continues to work on the problem with unconscious bisociation taking place. Many people say, 'I get my best ideas on the golf course, or in the bath'. Sometimes the strange and very welcome solution to a difficult problem appears in the mind when something totally different is being done. Incubation is used in a brainstorming session with the device of the 'Minute of silent incubation' (see next chapter).

Insight (Aha!)

Insight is the fourth stage of the thinking process. This is the flash of illumination which gives possible answers to the problem. 'Aha!', we say when we find those possible answers after struggling with a difficult problem. The flash of illumination is illustrated by the story of Archimedes, who had to find the weight and the volume of a gold crown. Archimedes was court scientist to the Tyrant of Syracuse, a suspicious man. He did not believe that he would ever be given a gold crown, and suspected there was lead and base metal in it. Archimedes knew the specific weight of gold and silver, and required the volume of the crown as well as the weight, in order to solve the problem. Some days later, he was taking a bath and noticed that the water level rose when he got into it. This was the flash of illumination he needed, and he ran the streets of Syracuse shouting 'Eureka' (Aha!). He merely had to put the crown into a bowl of water and measure the rise in the level.

Arthur Koestler, who wrote *The Act of Creation* (see Bibliography), has linked humour, discovery and art in what he calls the three domains of creativity. These are shown in Figure 1.3.

Humour	Discovery	Art
HAHA	AHA	AH

Figure 1.3   Three domains of creativity

The reaction to the three domains is given in the lower boxes. There is a deeper subtlety in this reaction than simply playing with the letters *A* and *H*. The reaction to humour — the ha! ha! reaction — implies an explosive release of tension. The good storyteller builds up the tension and holds the listener poised on the edge, until he states the punch-line. At once, or shortly afterwards, there is the explosive release of tension in the laugh. The reaction to art at the other end of the scale is the more gentle, emotional and controlled release of tension, as, for example, when studying the beautiful pictures in the art gallery, or looking at a gorgeous sunset. This gentler release of tension may also be accompanied by turning away, in case somebody sees the tear in the corner of the eye.

Evaluation

Evaluation is the final stage of the process. In this stage, all the ideas are analysed or evaluated to find the possible solutions. It can be a difficult stage and requires a good deal of persistence, particularly if the creative session has produced large numbers of wild or foolish ideas. The techniques of evaluation are discussed in Chapter 4.

A second look at the five stages shows that two of them are analytical. In the first, or preparation stage, although we are beginning to diverge, we are still using some analytical techniques to obtain all the facts. In the last stage of evaluation, we are quite deliberately converging to find possible solutions, and we use all the available analytical approaches. It is only the three centre stages of effort, incubation and insight that are the truly creative stages. In these stages it is necessary to suspend judgement and to put all the barriers on one side. The three stages require a free-wheeling, almost dreaming atmosphere in which bisociation and the interchange of ideas or cross-fertilisation can take place. Laughter plays a large part in these three stages.

This completes the look at creative thinking. The next chapter turns to the main technique in the creative field — brainstorming.

Solutions to problems

Student and the barometer

Other solutions include the following:

> Throwing the barometer from the roof, and timing its fall to the ground. The formula $S = \frac{1}{2} at^2$ gives the height (S) with a being the gravitational

acceleration of 32 feet/second/second, and t the time taken.

Standing the barometer upright, and comparing the length of its shadow with the shadow of the tall building — 'requires a sunny day', added the student!

Swinging the barometer as a pendulum at ground level and on the roof, and comparing the times.

Taking the barometer in to the building, and placing it against a wall, with base at ground level. Make a pencil mark on the wall at the top of the barometer, and lift the barometer until its base is on the pencil mark. Make another pencil mark at the top, and repeat until the roof is reached. Count the number of marks, the total is the height of the building in barometer lengths.

Present the barometer to the housekeeper, provided he will tell you the height of his building.

Scotsman and his dinner party

The Scotsman, in fact, had only to pay £70 for his party because the family consisted of two girls, one boy, their father and mother and the father's father and mother.

Solid wooden object

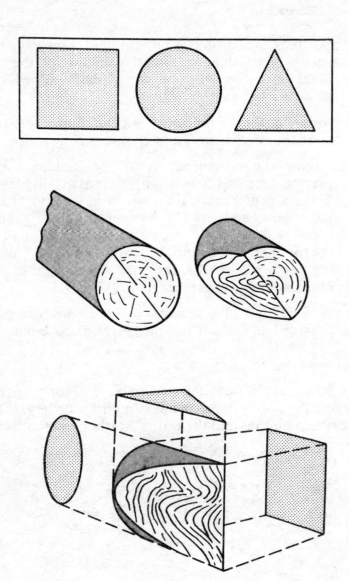

1 + 1 = ?

Answers include:

using the two '1s' — 11, X, L, V, T, = > , <

using the ' + ' and ' = ', — 7, VII, □, ┼┼┤

using all the symbols — ⁺╫╫ , ⊞ (a window)

⁺▢ (map symbol for a church, or a square woman upside down)

other way out ideas — Aye Aye, sight for a rifle, television aerial — and many others!

Nine dots and four straight lines

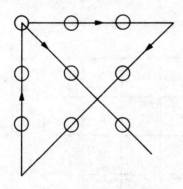

Nine dots and three straight lines

The solution depends on the dots having finite area, and the lines going through them at an angle

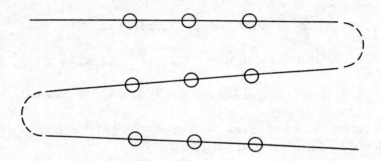

How many squares can you see?

A	B	C	D
E	F	G	H
I	J	K	L
M	N	O	P

Small squares	16)	
	)	
Four small squares, i.e. ABEF, FGKJ	9)	
	)	30
Nine small squares, i.e. ABCEFGIJK	4)	
	)	
Outside of squares	1)	
Frame, inside and including line thickness	2	
Thick line crossovers	25	
White squares and four thick lines	30	
White squares and two thick lines (four sets)	120	
Total	207 squares	

N.B   The last two assume that the thickness of the lines give an inside and an outside edge for each square, hence doubling the count of 30 squares, and giving an additional 120 squares.

Uses for a paper clip

The conventional use is clipping papers together, but there are so many other uses, and not all of them are wild or silly.
Examples are:

Pipe cleaner	Fuse wire
Nail cleaner	Tension reducer (fiddle with it)
Tie clip	Typewriter cleaner
Wax out of ears	Letter opener
Picture hook	Ornament
Poking holes	Repair for broken cufflink
Screwdriver	Poker chips
Toy tow bar	Missile for a catapult
Zip fastener tag	Daisy chains
Broken bra straps	Mobiles
Picking locks	Tooth pick
Fishing hook	

It is said that the paper clip was invented in the thirteenth century and has not changed since then, i.e. a piece of wire bent double at each end and folded in half.

2 What is brainstorming?

Brainstorming is only one of the weapons in the creative armoury available to managers. It is however the one most used — and most mis-used. This chapter and the next on procedures set out:

   to define brainstorming;

   to discuss the stages of a brainstorming session;

   to illuminate the 'tricks of the trade' in the running of brainstorming sessions; and

   to highlight associated techniques of restating the problem and wildest ideas.

Brainstorming, by its definition and its inclusion in the package of creativity techniques, is a wide-ranging, far-reaching activity, seeking to generate ideas. Because of the need to suspend judgement and to accept wild or silly ideas, a brainstorming session is almost out of control. Paradoxically, the control of a brainstorming session generates more, not less, ideas. This book sets out a systematic approach, which is almost guaranteed to achieve the very large number of ideas that normally appear in a brainstorming session.

Brainstorming has an honourable antiquity as a management technique. The technique was devised and used during the 1930s by Alex Osborn, in an advertising agency in New York (see *Applied Imagination* in the Bibliography). With the passing of the years, the word 'brainstorming' has become debased. It has been used to describe a group of people sitting round a table and throwing out ideas. This is nothing more than a bull session, resulting usually in a small number of not very good ideas. True brainstorming sessions are different, as this chapter and the next will show.

Definition

Brainstorming is defined as:

A means of getting a large number of ideas from a group of people in a short time.

The definition contains three aspects, a large number of ideas, a group of people, and a short time. First, a 'large number of ideas'. Notice ideas, the definition does not say good ideas. Brainstorming sessions that are well run will produce hundreds of ideas. These range from the brilliant winners to the totally wild, silly and useless ideas. All ideas are acceptable, indeed, the wild and silly ideas have a number of uses, one being to generate laughter. As we have seen in the last chapter, judgement is suspended and all ideas are acceptable. Laughter is an excellent catalyst — silence will kill a brainstorming session very quickly.

The largest number of ideas which I have obtained in a formal brainstorming session amounted to over 1,200. The occasion was provided by a small chicken-based food company who wished to diversify. The company was young, very successful, with a dynamic and thrusting management team. While the twelve hundred ideas contained many that the company was already using, and many that were quite inappropriate, some ideas were quite novel, totally appropriate and were adopted. Although this was the largest number, sessions producing six or seven hundred ideas are quite normal, and the shorter sessions giving two or three hundred ideas are quite commonplace. In another session, where the problem was how to reduce costs, one of the ideas was to sack Lord Blank, the chairman. While this was quite inappropriate (he was not present), it did serve to underline the free-wheeling nature of the session and the acceptance of all ideas in the atmosphere of suspending judgement.

A 'group of people', is the next important aspect in the definition. The optimum size for a brainstorming group is about twelve. In a group of this size, everybody has an opportunity to contribute ideas. The maximum size of the group should not be more than about twenty. In a large group the flow of ideas is so great that some people cannot get 'a word in edgeways'. After a while, they give up in despair and their contribution is lost. At the other end of the scale, a minimum number is about five or six, including the leader. A smaller group tends to be over-polite and to wait for each other to contribute ideas. It is also more difficult to develop a free-wheeling, laughing atmosphere in the smaller group. While a large group can afford to carry sleepers, who contribute little or nothing, the small group of five or six cannot afford this luxury. The 'sleeper' may have genuine reasons for not contributing. He may have serious family or business problems which he cannot shut out and these prevent him from really free-wheeling on the topic being brainstormed. This, and other aspects of the group such as composition, mix of ranks, are discussed in the next chapter.

'In a short time' is the final part of the definition of brainstorming. Many managers say they have no time to run a brainstorming session, they have to take decisions. Of course this is true, though in far fewer cases than the manager would care to admit. If a building is on fire, nobody would hang about to have a brainstorming session to decide what to do! But in my experience, the rate of flow of ideas in brainstorming sessions can be considerably in excess of 100 ideas in twenty minutes. The session with the food company mentioned above, which produced over 1,200 ideas, ran for about 3¾ hours.

The four guidelines

Success in brainstorming depends on the application and enforcement of four guidelines. All four were discussed in the last chapter, and need to be emphasised in any brainstorming session. They are:

```
Suspend judgement
Free-wheel
Quantity
Cross-fertilise
```

Suspend judgement requires that everybody, including the leader, should put evaluation on one side for the period of the brainstorming session. No evaluation is allowed, either of one's own ideas or those of anybody else. Anybody who does evaluate — for example, by saying 'that's a silly idea' — is forcefully told to suspend judgement. In the early stages the leader may have to enforce this, but as time goes by participants will themselves enforce this guideline, usually amidst some laughter.

Free-wheel means letting go of the barriers or inhibitions and allowing oneself to dream and drift around the problem. All sorts of ideas, good and bad, sensible and silly, are allowed and recorded.

The third guideline, *quantity*, may seem to be a misprint for quality. It is not. Quality has been put on one side with suspend judgement, and the participants are deliberately encouraged to produce a large quantity of ideas regardless of quality. All ideas are acceptable.

The final guideline, *cross-fertilise*, requires that ideas of other people are picked up and developed. In the normal analytical meeting, other people's ideas are respected and they are allowed to develop them themselves. Seemingly, it is impolite to take somebody else's idea and develop it. However, in brainstorming sessions, if another person's idea sparks off an idea in your mind, develop it, bring it out, and do not be angry if someone else develops your own pet idea. Cross-fertilisation allows the ideas to be exchanged, developed and changed by the group, under the control of the leader.

So important are these guidelines, that they are always put on display during a brainstorming session. Any participant not following them, e.g. failing to suspend judgement, is admonished by pointing to the displayed guideline. It may also be necessary for the leader to enforce the guideline, suspend judgement. If he does not, or he allows analysis or disapproval by any participant the free-wheeling atmosphere will break down. This is particularly important where the leader is not a senior member of the group. He must feel confident enough to enforce the guidelines on anybody senior to himself. This point is discussed in the next chapter in the section on the characteristics of a leader.

Stages of brainstorming

There are six stages of Brainstorming, as follows:

> State the problem and discuss.
>
> Restate the problem - How to . . . .
>
> Select a basic restatement and write it down, 'In how many ways can we . . .'.
>
> Warm-up session.
>
> Brainstorm.
>
> Wildest Idea.

Each of these stages is important and care should be taken to complete one stage before moving on to the next. This is particularly necessary in the third stage of selecting the basic restatement. The excitement generated in restating the problem may lead straight into brainstorming without a proper selection of the restatement and without writing it down.

State the problem and discuss

All the participants in the brainstorming session require to know some of the detail of the problem. While there will be some who know the problem in great depth — after all they have been living with it for some time — there will be others who will have only a vague idea of what the problem is. This stage of stating the problem and discussing it, is designed to give these people a minimum amount of information about the problem. A minimum amount is important — they need to know just enough to enable them to understand what the problem is, but not too much to be inhibited in their ideas for solving it. As will be seen the brainstorming group consists of a mixture of disciplines. Some are technically involved in the problem; others, who work in different disciplines, do not know about the problem, and it is these who are informed in the discussion at this stage. This can be seen as the insider/outsider contrast. Insiders, knowing the real detail of the problem and ideas already tried, will not put forward these or silly ideas. Outsiders do not have such knowledge, and will put forward ideas which insiders know will not work. But the insiders are unable to criticise because of 'suspend judgement'. So a limited amount of information, avoiding too much depth is given.

As an example, I was invited to run a brainstorming session in a company making oil seals for diesel engines. The problem was to find improvements to the oil seals. The chief engineer of the company who was present, had brought along a number of detailed machine drawings, and asked whether these should be put on display. The answer I gave was no, as these would give too much information to the non-technical outsiders, who were also present. The chief engineer was invited to describe the function of the oil seals, taking no more than five minutes on his description. A short question session followed, and the chief engineer was prevented from getting into too much detail about the technicalities of the oil seals.

Stating the problem and the discussion should be short, no longer than about ten minutes. Analytical questions and too much detail should be avoided. The problem should be explained by the person who has asked for the session, or by a participant who has knowledge of it.

In accepting the problem for brainstorming, it is important to take the 'problem as stated' by the person who has requested the session. He sees the problem in that way and can explain his view. It is little help to him to say, 'But that's not your real problem, your real problem is . . .'. He sees the problem in his way and will not take kindly to a blunt rejection of his view. Differing views are obtainable in the next stage, restating the problem, and it is here that all the different views should be obtained.

Restate the problem

This stage imagines the problem to be a large beach ball, two metres in diameter. Participants are encouraged to step back from it, climb over it, walk round it, and to identify as many different facets of the problem as they can. Each facet or restatement is phrased in terms of 'How to do something'.

The phrase 'How to . . .' has almost magical qualities in stimulating the flow of restatements. Note that restatements of the problem are required at this stage, not ideas nor solutions to it — they come later in the brainstorming stage. To ensure this, each restatement, including the words 'How to', must make sense in a literal way. If it does make sense, it's a restatement; if it does not, its a possible solution.

As an example, Chapter 4, p. 73-74, show the format for presenting the results of a brainstorming session. Two of the brainstorming ideas were: (1) Advertise, and (36) Credit cards. Although these were possible solutions, could they also have been restatements? Following the guideline of making sense in a literal way, the first — how to advertise — could also be a restatement. In fact it opens up all sorts of possibilities for solving the original problem. The second — how to credit cards — does not make sense and is therefore only a possible solution.

The distinction, and particularly the guideline of making sense in a literal way, may seem to be trivial and not worth following. In fact it is one of the real keys to successful brainstorming, for it is important to separate restatements and possible solutions. As many restatements as possible should be identified before attempting to find possible solutions. I have seen the two stages merged, resulting in fewer ideas from the brainstorming session, and even worse, whole areas of the problem being ignored.

Restatement and possible solution can be thought of as the two ends of a range or continuum. The point of change is not distinct and can easily be missed in the excitement of a brainstorming session. Indeed, as we have seen above, some restatements may also be possible solutions, in effect bridging the point of change. This is quite acceptable, provided that the restatement, including the words 'How to', makes sense in a literal way. The danger here is in drifting into the later brainstorming stage without completing the restatement stage. Forcing participants to make sense in a literal way is done by asking them to include the words 'How to' in their restatement. If it does not make sense, they can be asked to reword the restatement (including the words 'How to') until it does, or told to retain the idea as a possible solution for the later stage of brainstorming.

All the restatements are written down and numbered serially by the leader on sheets of newsprint so that they can be displayed to all the participants. Restating the problem should give at least twenty restatements, and may give as many as a hundred. As an example, I ran a brainstorming session for an overseas telecommunications organisation. The problem being brainstormed was, 'How can we make best use of the existing telecommunications system?' The organisation was worried that the existing system was obsolescent, and would be totally obsolete in a few years due to the technological advances in the communications field. After discussion, the group suggested eighty restatements, many of which were quite new and unthought of variations of the system.

Some restatements may appear to be mirror images of others. While in theory both are acceptable, mirror images should be discouraged, and the problem restated in a positive way. While restating the problem is the second stage of brainstorming, it is a powerful problem solving technique in its own right. This was mentioned in the last chapter in the preparation stage of thinking.

The leader should contribute restatements, and he may have prepared some before the session starts. The leader is a member of the group, and careful preparation may enable him to take the group into quite new and untried areas. From my experience, if the leader can prepare say ten restatements on his own before the session, a group in the free-wheeling mood generated will produce at least thirty.

Restating the problem is continued until participants dry up. The sheets of newsprint are displayed for participants to read, which can be useful in generating a few more. The next stage of selecting a restatement for brainstorming is then carried out.

While the use of the phrase 'How to' is important, in some circumstances it can lead to a wrong interpretation of the restatement. For example, the restatement 'How to identify new products', can place too much emphasis on the word 'identify' when the restatement really calls for a listing of the new products. In this particular case the word 'what' is added to the restatement, i.e. 'How to identify new products — what'. This ensures that the brainstorming session will not only identify, but also make a list of the potential new products.

Select a basic restatement

A number of restatements have now been written down on sheets of newsprint and put on display. The next step is to select one or two of these as a lead-in to the brainstorming session. There are two ways of selecting, 'autocratic' and 'democratic'. In the autocratic method, the leader himself does the selection. This can be appropriate, particularly if it is the leader's problem that is being brainstormed. The democratic method involves all the members of the group. In this method the leader asks participants to select up to seven or eight restatements which they consider to be appropriate in the light of the problem. Participants call out the serial number of the restatements, and the numbers are ringed or marked to distinguish them from the other restatements. After a few minutes when, say, eight restatements have been selected, the leader invites participants to choose the one or two which could be brainstormed first. Normally, one restatement is selected, but two or possibly three are seen as being close or linked to each other, and they can be put together as one restatement. The discussion of the restatement should be short and should avoid too much argument. The point here is that the participants are beginning to diverge and too detailed a discussion may become analytical.

When the first restatement, or restatements, have been agreed, the leader writes them down on the top of a new sheet of newsprint, prefacing them with the words, 'In how many ways can we . . .'. This wording is important as it takes the participants from the restatements to solutions, asking for solutions to be called out briefly so that the leader can write them down. There is a great temptation to avoid writing the restatement down and to jump straight into a brainstorming session. Excitement is being generated, and a free-wheeling, divergent atmosphere developed. If the restatement is not recorded, a participant may, at a later stage in the brainstorming session, lose track and wonder what the actual restatement is that is being brainstormed. He can work back up the list of ideas until he reaches the restatement and refresh his memory. If the restatement is not written down, he has to interrupt the session to ask the leader to remind him, bringing the session to a halt and interrupting the flow of ideas.

As ideas dry up on the first restatement, another is taken. It is not however necessary to brainstorm all the restatements. Using the beach ball analogy, a restatement leads participants into the beach ball, i.e. problem. The early ideas will be close to the restatements, but later ones will diverge and cover the whole problem. A second restatement should be selected as far away as possible (i.e. the other side of the beach ball) from the initial restatement. This restatement is written down on a fresh sheet of newsprint, and more ideas are generated, the serial numbers of the ideas being continued in sequence (see below).

'Warm-up' session

A warm-up session is placed in this position in the sequence of stages in the brainstorming session. It can, however, be used at any stage and is particularly appropriate at the start of the session to get the participants free-wheeling. Imagine you have invited a group of participants to a brainstorming session later in the week. When they arrive in the room, you notice that some of them hesitate and you realise they have forgotten to do something really vital, such as talk to an important customer, dictate an important letter. You need to turn them inwards to the session and make them free-wheel. You do this with a warm-up session.

A warm-up session is a short, not more than five minutes, quick-fire session in which participants throw out ideas. The key phrase is 'Other uses for . . .' — for example, other uses for a dining room table, a cigarette box, an ash tray, a glass, a pair of rubber gum boots. It does not really matter what the object is, the purpose being to generate ideas, serious as well as silly, and to develop a free-wheeling, laughing atmosphere. Another topic for a warm-up session, is 'Suppose you woke up tomorrow morning and you found that you, and everybody else, was half as tall (or twice as tall).' None of the ideas is written down, but a free-wheeling light-hearted atmosphere is generated. If necessary, a second 'other uses for' is taken and then the leader turns to the restatement to start the main brainstorming session.

Brainstorm

At the start of the brainstorming session, the leader reads the restatement(s) which have been written up on the sheet of newsprint, and calls for ideas. The flow of ideas should be fairly fast and the leader writes them on the sheet of newsprint as fast as he can. Each idea is numbered and when a sheet is full, it is torn off and put on display around the walls of the room.

There is one right way, and several wrong ways, to record the ideas. The right way is to record on sheets of newsprint with large felt-tip pens. Sheets of newsprint or rolls of ceiling or lining paper cut up to appropriate lengths, should be used — these can be clipped to a board on an easel. When the sheet is full, it is torn off the board and put on display. Displaying the ideas is an important aspect of brainstorming. Some authorities suggest using a flip-chart. This is quite acceptable, provided that the sheets can be torn off and put on display rather than flipped over, which is, after all, what its name implies. Recording the ideas on a transparency with an overhead projector is sometimes used. This is not to be recommended as only a limited number of ideas can be displayed at any one time. All the ideas must be displayed. A secretary to record the ideas should never be used. She is not part of the group, the ideas are not on display, and the participants do not know whether she is merely recording the ideas, or the name of the person suggesting the ideas as well.

Some books suggest that a tape recorder could be used to record the ideas. In no circumstances should a tape recorder ever be used. Once again, the ideas are not on display. Secondly, relatively few people are accustomed to being recorded and find the presence of microphones and tape recorder off-putting. In these circumstances, they will never relax and will not contribute ideas. Thirdly, the minute of silent incubation (see below) is hardly possible. A session which has been running for sixty minutes requires a sixty-minute play-back! Finally, and most important, unauthorised people may get hold of the tape. For example, imagine that you have just completed a very noisy, hilarious brainstorming session and have produced a large number of ideas, some of them very good, for solving a particular problem in the organisation. After the session, and still euphoric, you meet the chief executive who inquires rather brusquely what you were doing because the noise from the session interrupted all other work. You tell him that you were running a brainstorming session on a particular problem, obtained a large number of ideas and put it on tape. 'Oh, did you?' he says. 'May I borrow the tape?'

He may not know the finer details of the technique of brainstorming and he sits down to listen to the tape. The first forty or fifty ideas are all the old ideas that have been mulled over for some time and his reaction becomes slightly antagonistic. 'Oh, not that old idea again!' he says. Eventually at about number sixty a really wild or silly idea is put forward. He sits up with some shock because he does not understand the function of the wildest idea (see below). After several more wild ideas, he realises that these are being put forward by only one man, old George. At the end of the recording he may grudgingly admit to some useful ideas, but he declares that he will have to stop old George attending any more brainstorming sessions — he simply played the fool all the time. In fact, George was performing the very useful function of keeping the session light-hearted. For these reasons a tape recorder should never be used.

Sheets of newsprint with felt-tipped pens ensure that all the ideas are continuously on display. The growing list of ideas and the covering of all available wall space is a continual spur to the generation of further ideas. Putting the sheets on display can be a problem, particularly where large areas of fragile wallpaper or paint are used. Sellotape or masking tape should be tested on a dark corner of the wall to ensure that the surface is not removed when the sheets are taken down at the end of the session. 'Blu-tack' is a useful alternative and will do less damage to wall surfaces. Another more permanent arrangement in the brainstorming room can be to fix a thin metal strip at about picture rail height. The sheets of newsprint are attached to the strip with small bar magnets.

An important aspect of a brainstorming session is the generation of laughter and noise. The session that is totally quiet, apart from the ideas being put forward, will very quickly lose steam and die. Somehow laughter and noise seem to generate ideas and they should be encouraged. The leader can generate noise by repeating the ideas as he writes them down, by laughing with the wildest ideas as they are suggested, by calling for more ideas, e.g. 'Let's have some ideas', or 'Yes?', in a questioning way, and by occasionally repeating the restatement being tackled. As the leader will be writing the ideas he will be obscuring the sheet of newsprint. He should therefore, repeat the idea as he writes it down.

The method of writing the ideas down is a skill for the leader to develop. I have experimented with a number of different methods and find the best to be for the leader to write the ideas down himself. It is important for the ideas to come to the leader. He can shorten the idea to get it down quickly and in that shortening he may transmute it out of all recognition to the person who suggested it. This in fact, is a way of generating further ideas. When the participant says, 'I didn't say that', the leader's reply is, 'Oh, what did you say?' and generates another idea — two for the price of one. One suggestion is to have two writers. This does not inevitably increase the speed of recording, because the leader is able to repeat or transmute the ideas from the participant much faster than the writers can record them. In a little time the writers are left behind and protest, with the result that the whole session grinds to a halt.

Ideas are generated quite randomly by participants, although there may be some channelling when one idea opens up a number of similarly based ideas. This is to be welcomed, and no attempt should be made to take ideas in sequence, for example, by taking one idea from each person in turn. This will inevitably put 'old George' on the spot, when he cannot think of another idea. It is not good practice to embarrass participants — they simply dry up and resent being made an example in front of the others. Never turn to a participant and say, 'George, you haven't given any ideas yet, let's have one from you'. George does not have an idea, and resents being shown up.

As the session progresses, the rate of flow of ideas will fluctuate. After an initial fast flow the rate will slow down. There are several ways of coping with this slowing down and avoiding a total drying-up of the flow of ideas. One method is to have 'a minute of silent incubation'. In this, the leader calls for complete silence and asks the participants to read down the list of ideas nearest to them. The purpose is to cross-fertilise or spark off further ideas from those already generated. After one minute of complete silence, the leader repeats the current restatement and the flow of ideas picks up for another forty or fifty ideas. Another way to generate more ideas is to take a general idea stated earlier, and ask participants to state variants of it. For example, the idea, 'advertise' can be expanded to, 'Advertise on buses, on trains, in airports, on a balloon, etc.' The important point here is that all variations of an idea should be identified during the brainstorming session. No idea should be discarded because it is within another. It is only a repeat idea if it uses the same words (see below).

Finally, more ideas can be generated by taking another restatement from those selected earlier and writing it down on a new sheet of newsprint, repeating the phrase 'In how many ways can we . . . ?' Once again, the key points are to write the selected restatement on the newsprint, and to continue the sequence in the numbering of ideas. As a final resort, and particularly if the participants are not freewheeling and laughing, another warm-up session can be run on an outrageous topic to generate laughter.

The really important aspect is to keep the flow of ideas going and in this the leader can contribute ideas himself. The leader is a member of the group and is not debarred from contributions. This can be useful particularly where the leader wishes to change the direction of the group's thinking.

What happens in a brainstorming session if an idea is repeated? Instinctively, one writes it down again — the objective being to keep the flow of ideas going. However, there are some reasons for stopping and identifying the previous occurence of the repeat. A repeat is defined as an idea which uses precisely the same words as its earlier version. If different words are used, however slight the variation, it is not a repeat and is recorded. Locating the repeat allows a mini-minute of silent incubation — as participants look down the list of ideas to locate the previous version, they may cross-fertilise from the ideas they read. On finding the earlier version, the leader says to the participant 'Was that what you meant?' If the participant says 'Yes, it was', the session resumes. If it was not what he meant, the participant then suggests another idea, i.e. two for the price of one again. In addition, the repeat technique gives the leader an opportunity to relax — writing fast and long on sheets of newsprint with large felt-tipped pens can be very tiring.

There is no golden rule here. Either write the idea down without interruption, or stop and locate the earlier version. Remembering the repeat does, however, require the leader to develop a 'customs officer sense', which warns him that the idea has been suggested before. The procedure for a repeat is as follows:

Leader: 'I think we've had that one before. Can we locate it?'

Participant: 'Yes, there it is; number 139.'

Leader (to participant who is suggesting the repeat): 'Was that what you meant?'

Participant: 'Yes, it was', or 'No, I didn't mean that, I meant this ... ', and a second idea is generated.

When all efforts by the leader to generate further ideas dry up and the session is drawing to a close, the leader ends the session with the wildest idea technique.

Wildest idea

When ideas really have dried up, and the participants are feeling tired, having scraped the mental barrel, the session ends with the 'Wildest Idea'. This takes the wildest and most foolish idea from the brainstorming session and attempts to turn it round into some more useful ideas. As the wildest idea is usually funny, participants begin laughing again, free-wheeling and go away feeling that they have contributed some useful ideas. In addition, the wildest idea may lead to some excellent ideas which had not been thought of during the main brainstorming session.

Starting a fresh sheet of newsprint, the leader writes a heading 'Wildest Idea' and asks for the participants to select the wildest from the lists. At this stage, some ideas which originally provoked much laughter at their wildness, generate the comment 'Wait a minute, that's not so silly after all, we could make use of that idea'. When the wildest idea has been selected, usually amidst more laughter, it is written down on the newsprint and the leader calls for ideas for turning it into something useful. Usually ten or fifteen ideas are suggested, and these are recorded on the newsprint. Sometimes no new or good ideas are generated, although participants begin laughing again. In this case the session is ended as described below. Occasionally the wildest idea generates some very good ideas. In one brainstorming session on the topic of falling turnover in a hardware store, the wildest idea turned out to be 'a trap door in the pavement at the entrance to the shop'. Apart from its illegality, this is not a useful idea, but it was turned into a trap door in the wall of the shop. Tools requiring sharpening when the shop was shut could be 'posted' through the trap door with an indication of the work to be done, and collected a day or two later, when the shop was open.

There may be a call for a second wildest idea — and this can be taken. After it, the leader calls an end to the session, thanks participants for their co-operation and describes the next stage of evaluation (see Chapter 4).

Summary

These are the six basic stages in running a brainstorming session. Apart from the warm up session the sequence is important and should be followed. The six stages are: state the problem and discuss; restate, 'How to . . .'; select a restatement, 'In how many ways can we . . .?'; warm up; brainstorm; and wildest idea.

No attempt is made to evaluate any ideas. Evaluation is done later.

Several other aspects of brainstorming are crucial — the so-called 'tricks of the trade'. These are discussed in the next chapter.

3 Successful brainstorming

The last chapter defined brainstorming, and set out the six stages of a brainstorming session, including the four guidelines to be displayed. The six stages are only the bare outline, and experience has shown that further information is required by the manager wishing to introduce the technique into his organisation. For example, what factors should he take into account in selecting the people to invite to the brainstorming session? What are the characteristics of a successful leader? This chapter answers these questions, and gives some additional hints or 'tricks of the trade' for successful brainstorming.

Composition of the brainstorming group

The size of the group was discussed in the last chapter — the optimum being about twelve, with a minimum of five or six. I have run sessions with as few as three participants. Even though we were all motivated to derive ideas for solving the particular problems, the sessions were only partly successful. We felt that we lacked a breadth of experience on the problems, and that we needed some outsiders to generate wild or offbeat ideas.

In making up a group, the leader should insist on outsiders to the particular problem. There will inevitably be a majority in the group who are deeply involved in it, i.e. the insiders, but it is important that there should also be real outsiders. These outsiders do not need to be technically linked to the problem. They should come from other specialisms or technical divisions in the organisation and may include one or two from outside the organisation. If a production problem is being tackled, the group could include people from the sales side, people from the administrative or accounts areas, as well as a mix of production people who are involved and not involved with the problem.

An example from my experience is a brainstorming session on the marketing of cassette recorders. The organisation had a number of these cassette recorders which were highly priced and of relatively low quality and were having problems in selling them. The group consisted of technical insiders, an accountant and a manager from elsewhere in the organisation, two members of the trade press and a dealer selling the recorders. The last three were of course, well known to the technical insiders in the organisation. However, they provided a completely different viewpoint and contributed a number of useful ideas which the insiders had not considered.

The requirement of a breadth of knowledge and a range of experience amongst participants, suggests that ranks or levels in the organisation can be mixed. This can be one of the pitfalls and some care should be taken, particularly if the organisation is rather hierarchical or status-conscious amongst the various levels. The aspect here is that most important of barriers — fear of looking a fool — identified in Chapter 1. If the organisation is at all status-conscious, then the most senior and the most junior member of the group are afraid to let themselves go in case they make fools of themselves. The leader has to make a decision. If the organisation is not hierarchical, then some mixing of the levels is acceptable and easy. However, if some members tend to be status-conscious, then the leader should restrict the levels to one or at most two. Alternatively, he can deliberately invite more senior and more junior levels. In this case it is imperative that he should brief the most senior and the most junior so that they feel perfectly free to put forward wild ideas without being self-conscious about them. Extending this aspect of mixing the levels, brainstorming has been used to open up the channels of communication in organisations which are too hierarchical. The fun and laughter generated in a well-run brainstorming session will carry over into other meetings in the organisation. As a result, other more analytical meetings will be freer, possibly with more laughter and the phrase 'suspend judgement' being used.

If possible, the brainstorming group should have a mix of sexes. Men and women have different viewpoints on problems and it is useful to have all viewpoints represented amongst the participants. Approximately equal numbers of men and women are best, and the lone member of either sex should be avoided.

The mix of youth and age is generally covered by the difference in ranks. However, a mix of youth and age is to be recommended, with the younger being encouraged to put forward all ideas and the older being warned to suspend judgement, and to avoid such remarks as 'We tried that five years ago and it won't work'. The younger may have useful ideas to contribute, and the ideas of the older which were proved unuseable some years ago, may now be useable.

Another aspect of the composition of the

brainstorming group is the question of observers, and particularly non-participant observers to the session. This possibility arises from a request usually by a very senior person, phrased in this way, 'I don't know much about brainstorming, may I come along and watch?' The answer to this must be: 'No, not as an observer, but you are welcome as a participant'. Non-participant observers are not allowed in a session. They may inhibit the participants, who don't understand why they are present, and they may not accept the free-wheeling laughter generating atmosphere, as it is different from the serious (analytical) meetings they know. They may also be disturbed at the wild ideas, and be tempted to comment critically on those present. There is no reason why these senior people should not come along, provided that they are prepared to take part in the session. Briefing will be required particularly on the free-wheeling, wide-ranging nature of the session and on the instruction 'suspend judgement'. The latter is particularly important as these senior people may well have heard it all before, and know why a particular idea will not work. 'We tried it ten years ago', they say. In these circumstances, the leader has the responsibility of briefing the managers, ensuring that they participate in the session, and enforcing the 'suspend judgement' guideline where necessary on the senior.

The group should be given advance notice of the problem. The invitation to attend the brainstorming session, stating the time and the place, should include a one or two sentence description of the problem. Some participants may actively think about the problem and work out some constructive ideas. Others, generally a minority, may be deliberately antagonistic to the idea of brainstorming the problem at all. All, however, will take the problem into the subconscious part of the mind, where cross-fertilisation and development of ideas will take place. The information about the problem should be brief and should go no further than the title of the problem to be brainstormed and possibly one sentence of explanation. More detail, if necessary, is given in the first stage of stating the problem and discussing it (see Chapter 2).

The final point on the composition of a group relates to their experience in brainstorming. If a majority have not taken part in a brainstorming session before, then the procedure in Chapter 5 — 'Introducing brainstorming' — must be followed. However, if only a minority, say two or three, have not attended brainstorming sessions before, a brief explanation of how the session works will suffice with the newcomers picking up the free-wheeling, wide-ranging laughing atmosphere quickly.

Characteristics of the leader

As has already been said, the leader is a member of the group and must be prepared to contribute ideas. He is, of course, very busy running the session, ensuring that the six stages are followed, writing the ideas down on sheets of newsprint and enforcing the four guidelines. He should contribute ideas, and this can be valuable when ideas are drying up or he wants to take the group into areas not yet investigated. He must have attended brainstorming sessions and understand fully the way in which a brainstorming session should run, particularly the six stages and the four guidelines. He must have a genuine enthusiasm for the brainstorming technique and be prepared to share this enthusiasm with the other participants. A sense of humour is also important, for nothing is more contagious than laughter and enthusiasm. He must be able to generate noise, to write fast and visibly with large felt-tipped pens on sheets of newsprint, to spell and to count. He must also not be afraid of making a fool of himself in front of his colleagues.

While it is important for the barriers of the participants to be lowered, the leader should have no barriers at all. The wrong impression can so easily be generated by the leader ignoring an idea, or shrugging his shoulders at a silly idea. This quickly generates the impression, 'Oh, he doesn't want that sort of idea', and the barriers begin to go up. Having no barriers, or accepting all the ideas, however wild or silly, can be tedious for the leader. The group may be laughing uproariously at five, ten or fifteen really wild ideas which have no bearing on the problem. The leader must accept these ideas, and record them on the sheets of newsprint, even though he knows they are quite inappropriate. He must never try to stop the discussion by some such phrase as, 'That's a bit silly, isn't it?' Usually one of the participants will get tired of the silly ideas and suggest a good one. The leader should listen carefully for this and make an example in writing it down. Other participants will then crossfertilise from this idea and generate some useful ideas. This, in fact, has a bearing on the evaluation (see next chapter) for the wild patches of ideas may very well be followed by one or two winners.

The leader must enforce the four guidelines, particularly 'suspend judgement'. If the leader is senior to, or on a level with, the other participants, this provides no problem. If he is junior, then he must possess one additional characteristic — to be able to stand up to the most senior member of the group and enforce 'suspend judgement'. In the extreme example, where the leader is the most junior of the participants and the most senior begins to evaluate an idea, e.g. 'We tried that one last year and I know it won't work', the leader must firmly and courteously insist that the senior suspend judgement. The senior should enter into the spirit of the brainstorming session and this can generally contribute to the light-hearted atmosphere. If, however, the junior leader does not insist on suspending judgement, the participants begin to take the hint from the senior, start evaluating themselves, and the free-wheeling, divergent atmosphere is lost.

Practice by the leader will improve his skills in transmuting and writing down the ideas, and provide him with more time to contribute his own ideas as well. The first time of running a brainstorming session is the hardest, for he is standing out in front of his peers and possibly making a fool of himself. He must, therefore, have the will and the guts to have a go. It may be possible to develop a few members of the organisation in the skills in leading brainstorming sessions, and they can be called on to run sessions in various parts of the organisation. The leader does not need to be deeply involved in the problem — in some ways it pays to be an outsider. He must, however, do some preparation before the session. This preparation will include a detailed discussion with the originator of the problem to understand it, thinking about the composition of the group and issuing the invitations, and carrying out some preliminary restatements of the problem. In my experience, the preparation of ten to fifteen restatements by the leader leads to at least thirty in the live session.

'Tricks of the trade'

The success of a brainstorming session can be assessed in two quite distinct ways. The first way lies in the volume of ideas produced, many of which will appear later to be silly, wild, already being used, or just inappropriate. But it is volume, i.e. grand total number, of the restatements and ideas that is the basis of assessment without reference to quality. The second is a deeper way and, in the final analysis, is the real test. How many ideas are actually implemented? This is the ultimate objective of any problem-solving technique, and it is the ideas implemented that is the criterion, not the mechanism followed to find these ideas. Indeed, and quite rightly, the mechanism may well be forgotten in the euphoria of implementing a solution. So the first way, volume of ideas in the brainstorming session, is usually used as the criterion of success.

Using this criterion, there are a number of 'tricks of the trade' which can be used by the enthusiastic leader. While the word 'tricks' may smack of manipulation, this is not at all the intention. Purists may prefer the word 'technique' to describe the details which can lead to success. Unfortunately, the word 'technique' has also become debased, and many people claim to practise a technique when they do nothing of the sort. So I prefer the phrase 'tricks of the trade' to describe things the leader can do to stimulate the flow of ideas, and to keep control of a session which, by definition, is out of control.

Several tricks have been described in this and the previous chapter. They include the following:

Keep the six stages of brainstorming discrete.
Enforce the 'how to' of restatement by making sense in a literal way.
Display and enforce the four guidelines.
Have a group of about twelve, with a mix of insiders and outsiders.

Write restatements and ideas on newsprint and display on the walls of the room.

Generate noise and laughter.

Leader must be enthusiastic.

Use the repeat technique and the minute of silent incubation.

End the session on a high note with laughter at the wildest idea.

Several other tricks are available, and are discussed below.

The location of the brainstorming session is another important consideration for the leader. The best location is some neutral room or office, completely free from interruptions and without the distraction of a telephone. Nothing will destroy a brainstorming session faster than to have participants popping in and out of the session, or a girl from the office asking for Mr So-and-So to take a telephone call. Participants should be provided with comfortable seats only — tables are not required for notes will not be taken. Easy or comfortable chairs should not be shunned, there is little danger that participants will go to sleep in the excitement of the brainstorming session. In some cases, as has already been mentioned, a hat stand could be placed outside the room and participants requested to hang their barriers on it before the session starts.

Alcohol has been mentioned as a stimulant or a loosener of tension. While I have no direct experience of running a brainstorming session with the participants other than sober, I have used alcohol in one instance. This was in the making of the tape/slide training programme (see Bibliography). The programme includes an example of a brainstorming session which was made in a recording studio in a very tense atmosphere, quite strange to the participants. In order to relax, a bottle of whisky was opened and participants given a large slug before the session started! It is also of interest to note that in days of old, the ancient Goths debated important decisions twice, the first time when sober and the second time when drunk. This ensured that no vital matter had been overlooked.

A problem that may occur is the participant who 'hogs' the ideas and does not allow anyone else to suggest an idea. This can be aggravated if the participant is senior, and the others feel they have to defer, and allow him to continue. Eventually, of course, he will dry up, but by then the other participants may have switched off! The leader should listen for ideas from other participants, and emphasise them as he writes them on the newsprint. He can change the particular line being followed by injecting an idea himself, and calling on other participants to follow. Ultimately he may have to stop the participant by some phrase as, 'George, let the others have a go', or 'Fine, George, but can the others develop that last idea?' The leader must do this carefully and politely, and may have to face the accusation that he is not suspending judgement! In general, the best way is to allow the 'hogger' to exhaust himself. His ideas are probably sound, and he is one of the best producers of ideas.

The seats for the participants should be arranged in a U-shape to allow cross-fertilisation amongst the group, rather than the more standard classroom shape. The leader, with his sheets of newsprint, is placed at the open end of the U and should have access to the walls of the room on which to place the completed sheets of ideas. In order to keep the continuity and the flow of ideas, a member of the audience can be given the task of fixing the sheets up on the wall. Remember to test the wall surface if tape is used to attach the sheets.

Numbering each idea has two uses. First, the numbers can be used as a spur to obtain further ideas. For example, at 290 ideas, when the flow may have dropped off slightly the leader can say, "Come on, only 11 more to 300', and this will restimulate the flow. In addition, the location of a previous idea, as for example in the repeat technique, is considerably eased if all the ideas are numbered. 'There it is, number 156', the leader says. If the ideas are not numbered, the leader has to refer to a specific sheet and the particular location on the sheet which does not make for speedy location.

Another trick is to make the session open-ended. — Never state a finishing time in the invitation to participants. The point here is that a brainstorming session should end when the ideas really have dried up, and the leader has used all the methods of stimulating further ideas. If a specific finishing time has been stated, the session may dry up thirty minutes earlier or the ideas may be in full flood when the pre-stated finishing time arrives and participants have to leave for other engagements. If asked when the session will finish the leader should use such phrases as, 'You should allow about two hours', or, 'Don't fix anything for after the session. We may run on'. This will allow the time to be used most usefully, with the participants not feeling let down if the session ends early or runs on.

As a final comment on the 'tricks of the trade' the last two pages of this chapter give a list of 'Dos and Don'ts' in the running of brainstorming sessions. These are a useful reminder for the inexperienced leader, and a refresher for the experienced leader.

Perspective

This chapter and the last have described in considerable detail the methodolgy of brainstorming and the way to run a brainstorming session. Lest the reader should be carried away with enthusiasm for brainstorming and adopt it as the only problem-solving technique, let us restore the perspective.

First, brainstorming is simply one of a large number of problem-solving techniques and these techniques are both analytical and creative. All managers build up a kit of problem-solving tools and they are constantly adding to the kit. Add brainstorming to the creative side of the kit of tools.

The second perspective links with the first. While a brainstorming session *will* give a large number of ideas — in most cases many hundreds — it only *may* give winners. The correct perspective is to regard brainstorming and its associated techniques of restating the problem and wildest idea, as just another of the tools in the manager's problem-solving kit. Like any of the other tools, it cannot be guaranteed to give success, to give winners of ideas.

A third perspective is to realise that the brainstorming session is not the end of the process. In fact, the hardest part is still to come, that is evaluating the many ideas obtained in the session. This is looked at in the next chapter.

'Dos'

DO encourage noise.

DO encourage laughter.

DO allow wild and silly ideas.

DO write the ideas down on newsprint.

DO display the four guidelines.

DO enforce 'suspend judgement'.

DO suspend judgement yourself (when leading).

DO allow variations of ideas.

DO transmute ideas, to obtain two for the price of one.

DO identify repeats, the later version may be different.

DO identify barriers for newcomers.

DO brief seniors who take part.

DO number all ideas serially.

DO end on the wildest idea.

DO take other restatements when the first dries up.

DO write down each restatement — 'In how many ways can we ...?'

DO enforce the sense in a literal way in restating the problem, using the phrase, 'How to ...'.

DO have a warm-up session to encourage laughter and start free-wheeling.

'Don'ts'

DON'T ever tape record.

DON'T use blackboards or transparencies.

DON'T pick on 'old George'.

DON'T allow observers.

DON'T accept interruptions.

DON'T flip over completed sheets.

DON'T spend too long on the initial discussion, or allow too much detail.

DON'T drag out a session that has dried up.

4 Evaluation

This chapter looks at the procedures to be used in evaluating the hundreds of ideas obtained in brainstorming sessions. In some cases evaluation is simple and the good ideas stick out like sore thumbs and are easily identified. Unfortunately, these occasions are rare. Evaluation is a hard process, requiring a good deal of drive and persistence to identify the few good, amongst the many inappropriate, ideas. In addition, there is the danger that the few good ideas will be discarded, simply because they are swamped by the much larger volume of bad ideas. Some diligence is necessary to prevent dismissing all the ideas as useless, simply because the majority are useless or inappropriate.

Perhaps the problem of evaluation can be seen in a more realistic perspective with some facts. Assume that a brainstorming session on a particular problem has produced some 500 ideas. It was a wide-ranging, lateral thinking, free-wheeling session, full of laughter and enjoyment with all the ideas, no matter how wild, being accepted and written down on sheets of newsprint. Looking at the sheets of newsprint, or more appropriately, the typed list of ideas some days later, the impression is easily gained that there are no useful ideas and that the whole session was a complete waste of time. But this is a negative and destructive view. Put in another way, if one really novel idea or 'winner' appears in a brainstorming session lasting, say 2½ hours, that time has been really usefully spent. But in evaluation terms, one winner in 500 ideas means 499 losers! This is a measure of the pile of dross that has to be discarded before the nugget is found. Looking for a needle in the proverbial haystack can be easy, compared to finding the good ideas in the typed lists from a brainstorming session.

As has been discussed in the last chapter, a brainstorming session should generate a good deal of laughter and enjoyment in a really free-wheeling atmosphere. The process is divergent, with participants ranging far and wide in their endeavour to find possible solutions. Now comes evaluation of the many ideas. Evaluation is convergent, seeking to convert the many ideas into the few solutions. As such, it should be a cold, analytical process in which barriers go up, parameters are fixed and ideas which fall outside the barriers are discarded quite ruthlessly. Evaluation can also be time consuming, particlarly if there are no obvious winners and many of the ideas appear to be possible.

The above introduction to the procedures of evaluation may seem unduly pessimistic, or unnecessarily negative. In my experience however, considerable disillusionment for brainstorming can develop if the difficulties of evaluation are not appreciated and accepted. There have been occasions when the use of brainstorming in a slightly sceptical group of participants has been negated by the difficulties of evaluation. Looking at the list of ideas in the cold light of three or four days after the brainstorming session, the sceptic may say, 'There you are, I told you so. What a load of rubbish'. This, of course, is true — remember the 499 losers to find the one good idea. The danger of course, is in discarding the one good idea with the 499 losers.

Objectives of evaluation

There are two objectives in the evaluation process. They are:

> To identify the few good ideas and implement them.
>
> To demonstrate to the participants that action is being taken.

The first objective seems obvious. After all, brainstorming was selected out of the many problem-solving techniques available, to try and find an answer to a difficult problem in the organisation. The second objective is not quite so obvious. Participants leave the brainstorming session after the wildest idea, laughing and feeling that they have contributed to solving the problem. While this may be a false impression, generated by the laughter and enjoyment, the participants expect some action to follow. If little, or no action follows, the enthusiasm dies and participants will be reluctant to take part in further brainstorming sessions. In consequence, the leader should start the evaluation procedure within a day or two of the end of the brainstorming session. This will ensure that the momentum is maintained, particularly as the evaluation procedure may take some time to complete.

A 'do' and a 'don't' in evaluation

Before describing the procedure in detail, here are two hints — one positive and one negative.

DO wait a day or two before starting the evaluation. At the end of a brainstorming session, participants are tired and want to do other things. It would be quite wrong to start the evaluation process immediately, particularly as this involves analytical, convergent thinking. In addition, a gap of a day or two may generate more ideas in the minds of participants. These additional ideas may come from the unconscious, cross-fertilisation after the session or from the conscious development of further ideas from those generated in the session. These additional ideas should be welcomed and added to the main list.

DON'T ever evaluate with all the participants together in a live group. In such a group some participants may defend their own ideas, while the rest dismiss them as irrelevant or quite inappropriate. Bickering, argument and horse-trading develop and the creative value of the brainstorming session disappears. There is also another reason for not evaluating live in the group. Evaluation is time consuming and therefore expensive, relative to the brainstorming session itself. While a brainstorming session may take three hours, the time spent on evaluation may require three days spread over as many months. There is a way of involving all participants in the evaluation procedure and this is described below.

It is important to ensure that all participants know the outcome of the brainstorming session. This is partly achieved through the method described below involving all participants in the evaluation. Ultimately, when the evaluation is complete, participants should be informed by the leader of the action being taken and which ideas are being implemented. This should be done even if no useful ideas have been discovered.

Procedures for evaluation

There are two main methods of carrying out the evaluation. Both methods should be used, if only to involve all the participants, to avoid 'throwing the baby out with the bath water' and losing potential winners. The two methods are:

> Evaluation by all the participants.
> Evaluation by a small team.

Both methods are discussed below.

Evaluation by all participants

The first step in this method is for the ideas from the sheets of newsprint to be typed. With the very fast speed of writing by the leader, some of the ideas may be illegible. The list of ideas should therefore be edited and the illegible ideas interpreted for the typist. Editing should not include the removal of the very wild or silliest ideas — all ideas should be typed as they were

Table 4.1   Brainstorming session

Brainstorming session — 19 February 19__

PROBLEM   Turnover falling, and shops not as prosperous as they should be.

RESTATEMENTS How to . . .
1. Increase turnover
2. Reduce costs
3. Get more customers
4. Increase profits
5. Beat competitors
6. Sell more
7. Get people to buy more
8. Display better

9. Get customers to come back
10. Encourage big spenders
11. ...

etc.

BRAINSTORM

Restatements Nos. 3 and 7 were taken first and brainstormed.

In how many ways can we (3) get more customers and (7) get them to buy more ...

1. Advertise	31. Café upstairs
2. Prices down	32. Car park
3. Specialise	33. Pram park
4. Motivate staff	34. Crèche
5. Train staff	35. Drive-in shop
6. Better display	36. Credit cards
7. Open later	37. Cash cheques
8. Open Sunday	38. Cash only
9. Open all night	39. Credit
10. We never close	40. ...
11. ...	

etc.

WILDEST IDEA

278. *Burn the shops down*

321. Burn competitors
322. Burn a model of a shop
323. Sell fireworks
324. Check insurance

325. Sell central heating
326.   etc.

TOTALS		
	Restatements	45
	Brainstorm — Ideas	320
	Wildest idea	14
	Total	379

recorded. A typical format is shown in Table 4.1. The list starts with the problem statement as recorded on the sheets of newsprint and continues with all the restatements, headed by the phrase 'How to ...'. The first restatement(s) selected for brainstorming is then followed by the ideas from the sheets of newsprint, starting from number 1. Care should be taken to number the ideas in sequence with the numbers not necessarily corresponding to those recorded in the heat of the battle on the newsprint. If a second restatement(s) was selected, this is again typed and the subsequent ideas recorded with the numbering system following on. Finally, the heading 'Wildest idea' is typed. The wildest idea, with its serial number is recorded, followed by the subsequent ideas from the sheets of newsprint, the numbering system also continuing. At the end of the list, it is quite useful to repeat the total number of restatements and total number of ideas including those of the wildest idea, so that a participant can see at a glance the total number of ideas produced.

After checking by the leader, this list is then printed or photocopied and a copy sent to each of the participants. Each participant is asked to examine the list of ideas privately and without discussion with the other participants, and to select about 10 per cent of the ideas he considers to be useful, worthy of further and more detailed examination. The number 10 per cent is not significant and each participant may select more or less. After selecting the ideas, participants are asked to send the serial number to the leader. They should retain the list of ideas themselves, not only as a record of the ideas put forward in the brainstorming session, but so that they can refer to the list at a later date. Another look at the list of ideas in six or twelve months may reveal some which have become applicable in the meantime.

This stage can be quite time consuming, particularly as there will inevitably be some participants who do not do the selecting of their 10 per cent until chivvied by the leader. They may well be very busy, or absent on business or on holiday, or just plain lazy and put the list of ideas on one side to be looked at at a convenient moment. The leader may have to spend some time chasing these slower participants, in order that he may proceed to the next stage. Assuming that the list of ideas is in the hands of participants one week after the brainstorming session and the leader asks for the serial numbers to be returned one week later, it is probable that the collection will be done, not two weeks, but four weeks after the end of the brainstorming session.

As the participants return their serial numbers to the leader, they are recorded on the master copy of the list of ideas. Two things become immediately apparent. Some of the ideas — it may be as high as 50 per cent — do not receive any votes at all from the participants. These can be discarded. At the other end of the scale, some ideas receive many votes, possibly selected by every participant. By one sort of definition, these are the best ideas in the view of the participants. The leader, therefore, collects the ideas receiving most of the votes and puts these on one side as the best ideas.

There are a number of advantages in this method of evaluation. First, all members of the brainstorming group are involved privately in evaluating the ideas. No one is left out and all feel that they are taking part in a further stage of solving the problem. This process, in forcing the participants to pick out what they consider to be the best ideas, may give rise through cross-fertilisation, to further ideas which can be injected on to the main list by the leader. In addition, the list of ideas is out in public and participants may look back at a later date to the list and discover ideas that are applicable at the later date.

Evaluation by a team

The second method of evaluation involves a team of three or four of the brainstormers, including the leader. The team should be composed of people who are deeply involved with the problem and are committed to finding a solution to it. They will almost certainly be involved in implementation, regardless of the particular problem-solving technique used to tackle the problem. It may be possible to include one of the brainstormers who was an outsider to the problem. He must, however, have some special knowledge such as technical expertise, otherwise he will be unable to contribute to the selection of the best ideas.

The team tackles the evaluation in two stages. Working from the original sheets of newsprint, preferably fixed again to the walls of the brainstorming room, to give the atmosphere of the session, the team scrutinises the list of ideas and picks out those ideas which are obviously potential winners. This process can be quite short as the objective here is simply to select ideas which strike the evaluators as useful. It should not involve any detailed discussion. This comes later after the end of the second stage when the few best ideas have been selected.

The second stage starts by allocating each idea to a group of similar ideas, each group having not more than forty ideas in it. It is very much easier to evaluate ten groups of forty ideas, rather than one mixed group of 400 ideas. Remembering the problem and the general list of ideas, the team decide on the group headings and then run down the sheets of newsprint, allocating each idea to the groups. Some ideas may conveniently fall into two or more groups and they should be placed in each group. Once again, this can be quite short, the ideas being allocated to the groups without too much analytical discussion. Having allocated the ideas to groups, the leader takes the sheets of newsprint for typing. Each group has a separate sheet of paper, with the ideas allocated to the group typed on it.

When the typing is complete, the evaluation team reconvenes and each member is given a set of the groups of ideas. A number of criteria are agreed, by which the team may evaluate the ideas in each group. Some criteria are fairly standard and will appear in the evaluation of any brainstorming session. Examples are cost, time to implement, feasibility. Other criteria are specific to the particular brainstorming session and may, in fact, have been established before the brainstorming session starts.

The evaluation team then takes each group in turn and examines each idea with the criteria in mind. Initially, the criteria are applied negatively to eliminate ideas. For example, idea number 139 can be discarded because it is illegal. Idea number 236 would cost too much. After eliminating many, or most of the ideas in the group, the few that are left are then examined positively using the criteria to determine the best idea. Sophisticated procedures, such as ranking the ideas in order of priority, are not necessary at this stage. The purpose is simply to highlight the best idea or ideas, in each group. Having examined each group, the best ideas can then be arranged in a best ideas group and the criteria applied once again.

At the end of this stage, the evaluation team has three lists. These are:

> Best ideas from the individual participants, i.e. those ideas with most votes.

> The winners from the quick scrutiny of the lists by the evaluation team.

> The best ideas from the evaluation team.

These are again collated, and the best ideas are selected for further, deeper evaluation and possible implementation.

Two points should be stressed here. The objective of the brainstorming session in the first place was to identify solutions to the problems. If the procedure (brainstorming or evaluation) reveals possible solutions, they are immediately acted on. However, and this is the second point, it is still worthwhile carrying through the evaluation procedure, involving all participants and the evaluation team. This may reveal less obvious solutions, possibly of better quality than the original winners.

Time scale for evaluation

We have already seen that the evaluation procedure is time consuming — the evaluation by all participants may take up to a month. While the evaluation by the team can run concurrently, the final stage does require the evaluation from all participants to be available. In consequence, it may be up to two months before the evaluation has been completed.

Evaluation, therefore, does require some drive and persistence on the part of the leader to ensure that it is completed. In addition, there is the danger of dismissing all the ideas as rubbishy or totally inappropriate. As suggested above, the majority of ideas will be discarded and the formal evaluation procedures described above are designed to pick out the needle of a solution in the hay stack of ideas, or the tiny gold nugget in the large pile of dross. Remember the perspective, if only one solution is found in the evaluation, time on the brainstorming session will have been very well spent.

One additional trick may help the evaluation team in identifying possible winners. During the brainstorming session, there may have been patches of ten or twenty ideas which were completely foolish, inappropriate or wild but which caused a good deal of laughter in the session itself. These wild patches may be followed by some useful ideas as the participants in the brainstorming session become a little bit conscience-stricken at the wildness of the ideas and suggest good ideas which are totally appropriate. During the evaluation therefore, patches of ten or twelve wild ideas should be identified and the ideas immediately following, should be examined carefully as they may contain potential solutions.

Reverse brainstorming

After the evaluation has been completed, and the best ideas identified, these have to be implemented, or at least evaluated using other management techniques before implementation. Implementation may involve getting approval from higher authority and it is useful to subject each of the potential solutions to reverse brainstorming.

Reverse brainstorming asks the question, 'In how many ways can this idea fail?' This is sometimes known as the 'devil's advocate procedure'. Possible snags are anticipated, and answers are prepared for the awkward questions asked by the higher authority. Anticipating these questions, strengthens the case for implementing the idea and ensures that all problems associated with implementation have been anticipated.

Reverse brainstorming is carried out by the evaluation team and does not require the brainstorming participants to be collected together again. Reverse brainstorming is a useful technique in its own right and can be used outside brainstorming whenever higher authority has to approve a course of action.

The final step in evaluation is to inform the participants of the original brainstorming session of the results of the evaluation, and the action which is being taken to implement the ideas found. This can be combined with a word of thanks to the participants for the part they played in the original session. It will also remind them of the session and will tempt at least some of them to go back to the list of ideas, possibly generating other ideas.

Brainstorming and evaluation

Chapters 2 and 3 on brainstorming and this chapter on evaluation have described the main procedures in running a brainstorming session and evaluating the many ideas. These procedures can be summarised in Figure 4.1 The main stages in the brainstorming session

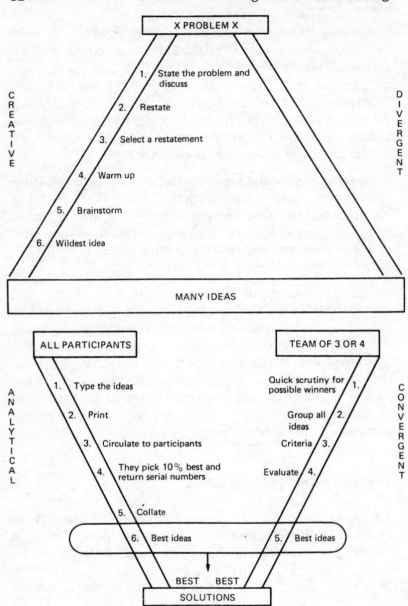

Figure 4.1   Summary of brainstorming and evaluation

are shown, and the two methods of evaluation. Notice that the brainstorming session is creative or divergent, resulting in many ideas. The evaluation is analytical or convergent and has its purpose in identifying the few solutions from the many ideas. The key to successful brainstorming lies in the conscious and deliberate separation of the creative or divergent stage of brainstorming and the convergent or analytical stage of evaluation. While analytical thinking should be deliberately excluded from the brainstorming session — remember 'suspend judgement' — there is no reason why some creative thinking should not be applied during the analytical stage of evaluation. In particular, there may be some cross-fertilisation or the triggering of new ideas during the evaluation process. These ideas can be quite properly added to the list and evaluated in the normal way. After all, the objective of running the session in the first place was to find solutions to the problem.

5 Introducing brainstorming

Like any other management technique, brainstorming needs to be carefully introduced to new participants. Apart from an understandable scepticism to a new management technique, there is a firmly rooted belief that existing techniques are quite adequate for solving the organisation's problems. It hardly seems to matter that these techniques are mainly analytical, and have not been over-successful in attacking the new problems which the organisation faces. In addition, brainstorming with its transatlantic flavour and a possible misunderstanding of the word — 'You didn't say brainwashing, did you?' — is increasingly misused. In a television programme some years ago, a group of police constables were invited to come into their senior officers' room for a discussion about a particularly difficult crime with the phrase, 'Let's have a brainstorm and see whether we can come up with some ideas'. Needless to say, the session bore no resemblance to a true brainstorming session. The constables simply sat round a table and discussed possible ideas in a very analytical atmosphere, and no one was very surprised at the lack of success.

It is an interesting paradox that a brainstorming

session is, by definition, out of control; yet a positive control exercised by the leader will increase the quantity of ideas obtained in the session. Participants range far and wide in their search for ideas. Control this search by the application of the tricks of the trade described in previous chapters, and the volume of ideas increases enormously.

It follows from the above that there is a right and wrong way of introducing brainstorming to new participants. The wrong way is to launch the participants straight into a brainstorming session on a live problem with only a sentence or two of introduction. For example, the leader may say: 'Let's have a brainstorming session. Here's what happens. You have to throw out ideas about the problem, no matter how wild, I'll write them down on this sheet of newsprint. The problem is . . .'. Participants do not really know what brainstorming is about, they apply their normal analytical routines and the session dries up after about twenty minutes with thirty ideas being produced. Participants go away saying, 'Well if that's brainstorming, I don't think much of it'. The only result of that sort of a session is that brainstorming, as a technique, is a non-starter. The right way to introduce brainstorming to a group of new participants is to go through two preliminary stages before a live problem is tackled. The first stage identifies the barriers to creative thinking and knocks them down. The second stage defines brainstorming and illustrates a session using a neutral example. Then, and only after the two stages have been completed, is the live problem tackled.

The first stage of identifying the barriers starts by defining creative thinking and showing the differences between it and analytical thinking. The barriers to creative thinking as discussed in Chapter 1 are identified, using examples such as 'the nine dots' or 'the squares' illustrated in that chapter. In addition, humour and laughter is injected into the session — the finest way of illustrating the definition of creative thinking is by humour, which also relates things or ideas that were previously unrelated. A method of demonstrating that the barriers have been knocked down is discussed later in this chapter.

The second stage defines brainstorming as a means of getting a large number of ideas from a group of people in a short time and discusses the four guidelines. A brainstorming session on a neutral topic is then run. In running this stage, I introduce the owner of a chain of ten hardware shops in which turnover is falling, and the shops are not as prosperous as he would like them to be. The participants adopt the role of being either shop managers or executives. Five of the six stages of a brainstorming session - discussion of a problem, restatement and selection, brainstorm and wildest ideas - are then run with tricks of the trade being discussed as they appear in the session. The session should run until at least fifty, or preferably just over 100 ideas have been produced. In discussing the definition of brainstorming and particularly the part which says 'in a short time', I inject the idea that participants will be producing 100 ideas in twenty minutes. The reaction, one of disbelief, is dispelled convincingly when the hardware stores example produces 55 ideas in eight minutes, or better still, 115 ideas in fourteen minutes. Both of these times are quite normal in my experience.

The philosophy behind this two-stage introduction of brainstorming is that the barriers to creative thinking have to be knocked down, the method of brainstorming has to be demonstrated and accepted, before it can be applied to a live problem. Experience shows that the barriers come down in the creative stage. They rise a little at the definition of brainstorming and in the hardware stores example and are held down, and rise again when a live problem is tackled. This is a natural progression, particularly in the last stage of tackling a live problem. Participants have been living with the live problem for some time and know the reasons why the solutions will not work. These past barriers are progressively lowered during the two free-wheeling, wide-ranging, laughter-generating introductory stages. For new participants to brainstorming, this introduction, which requires between 1½ and 2 hours, is absolutely essential.

The second and subsequent brainstorming sessions, with the same participants, do not need to repeat the two-stage introduction. Instead, a short introduction, say not more than ten minutes, is given in which the participants are reminded of the barriers to creative thinking, the four guidelines are displayed and emphasised, and the free-wheeling atmosphere generated by means of a warm-up session. Problems can arise if subsequent brainstorming sessions involve newcomers to the technique amongst the already trained participants. If a majority, say more than 75 per cent, of the participants have gone through the two introductory stages, then the short introduction can be lengthened slightly for the benefit of the newcomers who can pick up the free-wheeling atmosphere as the session develops.

If, however, more than one-quarter of the participants are new to brainstorming, it is important that the two introductory stages should be worked through. A separate session could be arranged for these people thus building up a larger number of participants who can take part in subsequent brainstorming sessions.

The development of a 1½ to 2 hour presentation on the barriers to creative thinking, and hardware stores example from the material in Chapters 1 to 3, is relatively simple. There is however, an additional way referred to in the Bibliography. This is the tape/slide programme which I prepared with Management Training Limited, now a part of Guild Sound Services. The programme consists of a leader's guide, some 72 slides, a stand-up card with the four guidelines and a reel-to-reel tape. The leader's guide includes a transcript of the tape with indications of where the tape should be stopped for a discussion of the problems posed. The barriers to creative thinking are identified and the hardware stores example is illustrated on the tape with the first twenty ideas of the session. The leader is then invited to take over and continue the session for as long as he considers it to be necessary and before starting on his own problem.

Can creativity be taught?

In the wider context of creativity in art or science, this question is appropriate, but is outside the context of this book. In the narrower context of brainstorming, the real question should be: 'Can creativity of managers be improved?' As has been stated in Chapter 2, I believe that all managers have an innate creative ability which they do not use enough. This ability was there when they were children, but has been gradually stifled as they grew up by the analytical procedures taught in schools, university, technical or professional training and in the various levels of management. At every stage, creative ideas tend to be discouraged and the analytical approach or one right answer encouraged. In other words, the barriers identified in Chapter 1 have been built up and it is these barriers that have to be removed before participants can usefully take part in brainstorming sessions.

So the question 'Can the creativity of managers be improved?' could more appropriately be rephrased to 'Can the barriers to creative thinking be removed?'. I have no doubts about the answer to this question — it is a categorical yes. I am sure that the barriers to creative thinking, outlined in Chapter 1, can be identified by managers, accepted (possibly with some reluctance) and removed.

In Chapter 1, p. 11 on the barriers to creative thinking, you were asked to imagine an ordinary paper clip and to jot down good uses. After identifying the barriers, particularly the fear of looking a fool, you were invited to go back to the list and add further ideas — it is hoped that you more than doubled the list. In a live presentation on the barriers, I have extended this idea by using two objects, a paper clip and a man's leather belt.

The procedure for the paper clip and man's belt is as follows. At the start of the discussion on the barriers to creative thinking, I show a paper clip and ask participants, 'In the next two minutes, write down as many good uses for this paper clip as you can, and I will ask one of you to read out your list'. During the two minutes, 'good uses' and 'read out your list' are emphasised. After two minutes the participants are asked to add up the numbers of uses they have written down, and the numbers, usually from ten of the participants, are recorded on a sheet of newsprint, totalled and averaged. The sheet of newsprint is then put on one side with the assurance that it will be examined again later in the presentation. After discussing the barriers and knocking them down, I show a man's leather belt and invite participants, 'In the next two minutes, write down as many uses as you can think of for this man's belt. Suspend judgement — put down all the ideas you can think of, good, bad, useful, useless, legal, illegal, it doesn't matter, put them all down'. During the two minutes, 'as many uses' and 'suspend judgement' are emphasised. After two minutes the participants are asked to add up the numbers of ideas. The same ten people are taken usually in reverse order to avoid invidious comparison and the numbers recorded along side the numbers for the paper clip. The numbers are again totalled and averaged.

The results from this exercise are quite striking. Over four years to the end of 1979, I collected the results from over 200 presentations or seminars giving just under 2,200 pairs of numbers of uses for the paper clip and man's belt. In most cases the sequence was paper clip first followed by the man's belt. But on a small number of occasions the order was reversed taking the man's belt first ('good uses' and 'read your list out' being emphasised), followed by the paper clip ('as many uses' and 'suspend judgement' being emphasised). The result in these cases was just as striking.

The results were as follows. In the standard order of paper clip first:

Histograms for the two sets of uses peaked at 4 for the paper clip and 8 for the man's belt.

Overall averages were 4.9 for the paper clip and 8.6 for the man's belt.

51 per cent of participants gave 3, 4 or 5 uses for the paper clip, and 53 per cent gave 6, 7, 8 or 9 uses for the man's belt.

Uses for the paper clip ranged from 0 (on two occasions!) to 15, with one at 18 uses. Uses for the man's belt ranged from 1 to 21, with one at 23 and one at 25 uses.

In the reverse order of man's belt first followed by the paper clip, and with smaller numbers (71 pairs);

Histograms peaked at 4 for the man's belt and 7 for the paper clip.

Overall averages were 5.9 for the man's belt and 10 for the paper clip.

Uses for the man's belt ranged from 2 to 11, with two at 15. Uses for the paper clip ranged from 4 to 17, with one at 20.

One other interesting result appeared from the records. More uses on the second occasion was not universal. In fact on 5.5 per cent of the occasions the same number of uses was found, and on a further 5.3 per cent of the occasions less uses were found on the second occasion, the predominant figures being one or two less uses.

These figures from the paper clip and man's belt examples were obtained in seminars in the UK, and in many countries around the world. They appear to bear out the conclusion that creativity in managers can be improved. I wonder how many more uses you added to your list for the paper clip in Chapter 1? (Some additional results with comments are given in the next chapter.)

However, a careful reading of the instructions for the paper clip and man's belt may lead to the realisation that the instructions in each case were different. This is quite deliberate, because I make an additional use of the comparison — to demonstrate the biggest barrier of all, fear of looking a fool. On the first occasion — paper clip or man's belt - the instruction included the phrases 'good uses' and 'read out your list'. Participants think of a use, consciously or unconsciously, evaluate it as quite silly or inappropriate, and do not put it in their list. In fact this was the reason given by the two participants who could not think of a single good use for a paper clip — they would not use paper clips for holding papers either, even though they are designed to do just that! When asked to add up the number of uses, I avoid asking anyone to read out their list, and so nobody is made to look foolish. Later, on the second occasion — man's belt or paper clip — no mention is made of reading out a list, and the participants therefore feel quite safe to write down all sorts of uses, good and foolish.

While the changing of the instructions may damage the strict validity of the comparison of the figures, I believe that the large increase in uses, and the same picture being found when the order is reversed, demonstrate that the barriers have been recognised and lowered.

One other factor contributes to the successful introduction of brainstorming in an organisation. This is the enthusiasm of the leader, both for the technique and for the group tackling the problem. Nothing is as infectious as enthusiasm, and the leader should possess it in abundance.

6 For instances

Since 1966 I have given more than 700 talks and seminars on creative thinking and brainstorming. These have ranged from half-day sessions on training courses, to two-day brainstorming sessions with companies to tackle particular problems. The latter have always included an introductory discussion on the barriers to creative thinking and on brainstorming, using the hardware stores example described in the last chapter. In all the sessions an objective has been to pass on 'tricks of the trade' so as to enable managers to introduce and run brainstorming sessions in their own organisations.

Several example or 'for instances' have already been discussed in earlier chapters. This chapter extends these by discussing further examples in:

The barriers to creative thinking

Brainstorming

Wildest idea

Evaluation.

Barriers to creative thinking

The barriers to creative thinking have been identified in Chapter 1. Chapter 5 on introducing brainstorming seems to reach the clear conclusion that creativity can be improved, provided certain conditions are met. One of these is the complete separation of analytical from creative thinking — most people analyse new (creative) ideas far too quickly, and do not give them a chance to grow. By consciously suspending judgement, the barrier of evaluating too quickly is removed. The phrase, 'I wouldn't dream of doing that', has no place in the language of the creative man.

Nonetheless the barriers have to be recognised and lowered before most managers will allow themselves to freewheel. In the last chapter, the results of the paper clip/man's belt examples were given. One additional result, not quoted, was that 79 managers could think of only one good use for a paper clip! This was nearly 4 per cent of the occasions recorded, and is an astonishing commentary of the creative ability of managers — or the lack of it.

In terms of an organisation rather than individuals, one company in which I introduced brainstorming gave an interesting commentary on its creativity. On tackling the paper clip, five of the fourteen managers — top management in the company — could only think of 1 use of a paper clip and three more managed only 2 uses. The average for the group was 3 uses for the paper clip, with the highest at 8 uses. The creativity was latent. After discussing the barriers, the group averaged 7.6 uses on the man's belt, ranging from 3 to 12 uses. The biggest improvement was from 1 use on the paper clip to 10 on the man's belt.

As mentioned in Chapter 5, the results on the paper

clip/man's belt examples seem independent of age, culture, seniority, and technical specialism. The figures were recorded in sessions in the UK, Europe, Venezuela, Nigeria, Malaysia and Hong Kong. They covered a wide range of managers in public and private sectors, industry and commerce.

Another barrier is the feeling that one answer is enough, particularly if it conforms to an obvious pattern. The A B C D E pattern in Chapter 1 is an example. Many people choose one and are somewhat dismayed to find the second, quite accurate, pattern.

I had an interesting example of barriers when a very senior, recently retired and much respected works manager asked if he could attend a session for some fifteen managers in his works. After the usual introduction on the barriers to creative thinking, and on brainstorming, a factory problem was brainstormed. The very senior works manager was carefully briefed before the session as to what would happen, and what he should do (including suspending judgement), all of which he accepted. During the brainstorming session he could not hold himself back and said, 'I've been listening to all the ideas you've been producing. I hate to tell you but I've tried them years ago, and I know they won't work'. To give him his due, he accepted with great good humour, the shout of 'suspend judgement' from the remainder of the brainstormers. Later he admitted that one or two of the ideas might be feasible now — they were not when he had tried them!

Brainstorming

In commenting on brainstorming, two different values can be used — the volume of ideas produced, and the usefulness of the session in generating solutions to the problem. Volume is only a rough measure, for the objective must be to find solutions to the problem. It does, however, indicate the well of ideas which exist and which could be tapped with considerable benefit to the organisation.

The example of the chicken-based food company producing over 1,200 ideas for diversification was mentioned in Chapter 2. While this is a maximum in any of my brainstorming sessions, achieving hundreds of ideas is quite commonplace. Some examples taken from a range of sessions are:

> A consulting company brainstormed the buying motives of clients for the various management techniques. In one session a group identified 646 motives for seven techniques. Later a second group identified 723 motives for five techniques.

> A company wondering about supplying management information for the sales and marketing staff identified 489 ways in which this could be done.

> A company using van salesmen identified over 400 products which could be added to the range. These included bought-in products as well as those made by the company.

> A company in a seasonal business identified 650 ways of keeping the works busy in the slack periods. While many were quite inappropriate, several were adopted and provided a useful contribution to the company's profit.

> A company producing a new photocopier ran a series of brainstorming sessions on its possible use within the company and with large potential customers. In six sessions a total of 183 restatements and 2,024 ideas were produced. While

there was some inevitable overlap in the six sessions, a considerable number of novel uses were identified for deeper investigation.

A multinational company seeking to improve on and intensify the company's search for new industrial activities produced over 400 ideas.

A paint company used brainstorming to identify ways in which architects could be persuaded to specify their paint to customers. Just under 300 ideas were produced.

In all these examples a preliminary introduction had been given. This covered the barriers to creative thinking, and the hardware stores example to demonstate how a brainstorming session was conducted. The groups comprised managers at various levels in their companies, few of whom had met any creativity techniques before the session. I ran the sessions and was able to generate much enthusiasm in the ideas of creativity and for brainstorming as a technique. But it is not necessary for the expert to run the session. I have been present at, and guided, many sessions which have been run by one of the participants after the standard introduction. In all cases hundreds of ideas were produced.

Other examples of brainstorming sessions, with a comment on the usefulness of the ideas produced are:

A small company had introduced a management by objectives programme some six years previously. While the programme was very successful and gave good results, management felt that it needed updating and rejuvenating. Three separate groups of managers and foremen brainstormed to identify improvements. Eliminating repeats, over 150 ideas were produced for improvements in job specifications, performance plans, appraisal and counselling reviews, controls and communication. Apart from identifying major improvements in the paperwork, all agreed that the programme had been given a useful new lease of life.

A car accessories firm used brainstorming to identify 437 ideas for new products. During the session, it was realised that a car boot is a much neglected area of the car, and worthy of custom-built accessories.

A newspaper used brainstorming to identify ways of reducing costs. Over 600 ways were identified, including the shutting down of two out of six printing presses. Afterwards the production director commented that he would not have dared to suggest that idea to the unions. The group had included some union officials, and the production director proposed to talk with them on the possibility of shutting presses, 'as it had been suggested in the neutral atmosphere of a brainstorming session'. Another idea had been to print the business news section as part of the paper, and not as a separate insert as was the current practice. This was also adopted.

During the UK postal strike some years ago, a local political party used brainstorming to tackle the problem of circulating the notices for the annual general meeting. This would have had to be postponed if notices were not issued some days before the meeting. One idea in the session was to make use of local milk roundsmen. They would know the political allegiance of their customers, and could hand the notices in to the appropriate houses.

A major company had a stock of 470 cassette recorders to sell within a year. The problem was that these recorders were relatively highly priced and of low quality, with the resulting low sales. Nearly 600 ideas were produced, including several which were adopted, resulting in the successful sales of the recorders.

When I was a member of staff at Sundridge Park Management Centre, I ran a brainstorming session on the design of the brochure giving the details of all the courses. Over 250 ideas were produced, including one of a centrefold picture of the tutorial staff. This was adopted and extended to include a picture of one of the buildings with groups of all the staff. The tutorial staff were placed in a prominent position in the centre of the picture.

A company in the building industry used brainstorming during a three-day director's meeting to consider the future of the company. At various stages during the discussions, I ran short brainstorming sessions on topics such as:

how to entice people to join the company;
company strengths and weaknesses;
markets which will grow and which will decline; and
what to do with present resources.

The ideas were typed and given a preliminary evaluation during the meeting, followed by a deeper evaluation over the ensuing months.

A company used brainstorming to check on the design team's proposals for a new piece of electronic equipment. The brainstorming group included only one or two members of the design team and produced no new ideas. Far from being disappointed, the head of the design team was delighted, for it showed that all possibilities had been thought of, and the design team had done a good job.

A company had introduced a productivity deal for the works. As part of a weekend get-together for all managers down to the shopfloor, brainstorming was used to consider the problem of 'increasing the share of the cake in the productivity deal'. Three groups, run by members of the company, with my guidance produced over 900 ideas. While there was some triplication of ideas in the groups, over 100 were selected as worthy of additional scrutiny and evaluation.

These examples demonstrate the usefulness of brainstorming as a technique for generating ideas.

Wildest ideas

As explained in Chapter 2, the wildest idea technique is used at the end of a brainstorming session to turn the wildest idea into useful ideas, and to generate laughter.

When I introduce creative thinkng and brainstorming to a group of managers who are new to the technique, a demonstration of brainstorming is always given. This is usually the hardware stores example, being a neutral example in which no managers are deeply involved. During these sessions wild, and sometimes very wild, ideas are obtained. The wildest idea technique is always demonstrated using one or more of these. The example of the trapdoor in the pavement has already been mentioned in Chapter 2. Other examples from sessions are:

Burn down the shops — leading to burn the competitors, knock competitors, steal competitor's staff, check insurance first, burn a model of the shop as advertisement, and a bring and burn sale.

Throw nails in road to stop traffic — leading to a bus stop, give away nails, advertise on buses, window display on first floor for upstairs passengers on the bus.

Window undresser — leading to stripper in the window, sell paint strippers, weekly window change, demonstrations in the windows.

Sell vice — leading to selling clamps, good service, DIY advice and vicycle clips.

Some of the ideas were unprintable, and almost automatically became the wildest. This generated laughter at the end of the session, and on occasion were turned into winners.

These were all in the demonstration of how a brainstorming session should run and arose in the hardware stores example. Some examples from sessions on live problems in companies are:

A company ran a brainstorming session on the problem of rewarding the best salesmen in a team. A wild idea was 'a trip in Concorde', which was turned into a visit to the company's American headquarters.

The chicken-based food company mentioned in Chapter 2 produced a wild idea 'kill-a-chicken day.' This was turned into date coding to show when killed, a chicken calendar, 365 recipes for chickens and recipes for chicken left-overs.

The overseas telecommunication organisation

mentioned in Chapter 2 produced a wild idea, 'feelies and smellies by wire'. This was turned into braille by wire, pollution monitoring, lie detectors by phone, tele-doctor, frost warning, and smoke warning in a burning house.

A printing company in a country location produced a wild idea of 'fattening turkeys in the litho hall' when business was slack. This was turned into printing materials for the turkey trade, i.e. labels, packing, price tags, and printing immigrant literature.

A company making carbon paper brainstormed future markets and products. A wild idea was 'edible carbon paper'. This led on to selling carbon paper in grocers shops and bakeries, and making carbon paper suitable for restaurants and cafés.

A shoe company used brainstorming to get ideas for new products. A wild idea on new materials was to use 'eyeballs' from the slaughter houses where the leather originated. This led to a reflective material on the shoes to show up in the dark, and a material incorporating a cleaning device like an eyelid.

A biscuit manufacturer used brainstorming to develop ideas of coping with very high labour turnover. As biscuit-making leads to scrap, the idea of liqueur biscuits was developed from the wild idea of parties in which the staff trod on grapes put into the piles of scrap biscuits.

A brainstorming session in a brewery on cleaning of vessels and pipes produced the wild idea, 'bring back cats'. This led to mechanical moles pushed through the pipes with detergent and sterilising chemicals attached.

A fast food company with car parks for visitors had the wild idea of 'walkie-talkie radios for communicating orders'. This led to equipping the car park attendants with walkie-talkies so that customers could order from the car park, and find their meal ready when they arrived in the restaurant.

Presented formally as above, the ideas do not seem to be particularly wild, nor do the subsequent ideas appear to be winners. They did generate laughter in the brainstorming session, and again at the end when participants were tired. Some of the follow up ideas were adopted.

Evaluation

As discussed in Chapter 4, evaluation is the hardest and most demanding part of a brainstorming session. It can be time consuming, and give some disillusionment to the process, especially when nothing seems to be happening with the ideas produced. The three stages of quick scrutiny, evaluation by all participants and evaluation by a team should always be used.

In the brainstorming session mentioned above on the design of the brochure for Sundridge Park Management Centre, several ideas stood out as potential winners and were immediately followed up. The full evaluation process took several weeks to complete, mainly due to the time taken in following up the individual evaluations.

In another example where a series of brainstorming sessions were held during a three-day conference, the ideas produced in the conference were evaluated over a six-month period. Several meetings of working parties were required to examine and develop the ideas.

Another company brainstormed its future, looking at products and processes. Over 350 ideas were produced, and some three months elapsed before these were reduced to four for implementation.

In the cassette recorder example mentioned above, the second day was spent in an initial evaluation. This produced some ideas which were immediately implemented. Further and deeper evaluation was done over the following weeks, and further ideas developed.

These four examples illustrate that time and effort are required in evaluation, and some persistence on the part of the leader is essential to complete the process. Like most techniques, there is no easy way to the best solution. Brainstorming will give very many ideas. It only may give winners, and some patience is required to follow up all the ideas. Of course the obvious winners of ideas are implemented quickly without waiting for the completion of the evaluation. But these may not be the best ideas, and the complete process is always worthwhile.

7 Related techniques

While brainstorming, with its associated techniques of wildest idea and reverse brainstorming, is the most used and the most useful technique in the creative field, there are others. They are not as widely known nor as well-used as brainstorming, but they do have their uses and no book on creative thinking would be complete without a mention of them. This chapter describes the techniques briefly and indicates some uses.

The main techniques discussed are:

Synectics

Attribute listing

Forced relationships

Morphological analysis

Lateral thinking and PO

Check lists.

Synectics

(With acknowledgement to Abraxas Management Research of Worcester Park, Surrey. Abraxas are the UK associates of Synectics Inc. of Cambridge,

Massachusetts, USA). Synectics is an idea-generating and problem-solving technique which originated in America in the late 1950s with the work of W.J.J. Gordon and George Prince. Together they founded Synectics Inc. in Cambridge, Massachusetts, and licensed users in many parts of the world.

A synectics group consists of a leader, a client and about six participants. The leader is responsible for running the session and for recording all the ideas produced on sheets of newsprint. He is concerned solely with the process of synectics and ensuring that it is conducted correctly. As such, he is specifically barred from getting involved in the content of the session and does not contribute ideas himself. The client has the problem and the process is directed to producing acceptable solutions for him. In the process, the client's requirements have to be satisfied and if he does not wish to investigate an avenue, he has the right of veto. The participants need not be technically involved with the problem and the process seeks to commit the client to taking action on the solution generated. The process involves short bursts of analytical and creative thinking and aims for a solution in about 45 minutes. Each burst of analytical or creative thinking lasts no longer than about 5 to 10 minutes and the client is continually referred to in order to ensure that the avenue being investigated is acceptable to him.

The synectics process has a number of stages as follows:

Problem as given (or PAG)

Analysis

How to ...

How to: selection and mini-analysis

Idea

Paraphrase

Itemised response

Possible solution and next step.

Problem as given (or PAG)

The client, whose problem is to be discussed, gives a one sentence statement of it. The statement is written down on a sheet of newsprint for all participants to see, using the precise words of the client — hence the problem as given, or PAG.

Analysis

In this stage the client gives the background to the problem, ideas that have been thought of and tried, and also describes whether he has the power to act on any solution produced. He gives an indication of any ideal solutions, stated in the form of 'It would be nice if . . .'. During this stage, the other participants listen actively and make notes of any points that occur to them. These points could be immediate ideas for solving the problem, alternative definitions of the problem, challenges to the client's point of view. The two stages of PAG and analysis should take no more than about five minutes.

How to's (or H2)

In this stage, the participants and client restate the problem in terms of 'How to . . .'. Headlines of each 'how to' are recorded by the leader prefaced by 'H2'. The participant or client comment on the background thinking, giving the leader the time to write down the restatement on the sheet of newsprint. Evaluation is not allowed and some 25 or more restatements encouraged. This stage takes up to 9 minutes.

How to: selection and mini-analysis

When sufficient restatements have been obtained, the leader invites the client to select one or two restatements which appeal to him as potentially useful. The client indicates why the ideas appeal to him and states what further help he needs. During this stage only the client talks, the participants listen actively and note down any ideas they may have.

Idea, paraphrase and itemised response

These three stages constitute the main part of a synectics session and are known as idea development. The leader asks the participants to contribute ideas on the selected 'how to' restatements. Any participant may contribute ideas, and the others may build on it, within the framework of the 'how to' statement. After a few moments the leader asks the client to paraphrase the idea to ensure that he accepts it and that no aspects have been misunderstood. Participants may also correct any misunderstandings. When the leader is sure that the client understands the idea, he asks for three itemised responses. These force the client to state the good points of the idea (i.e. the useful, helpful aspects). The client also points the direction in which he wishes the idea to be developed with a further 'how to' statement, amplified with his background thinking.

These three stages of idea, paraphrase and itemised response are repeated a number of times until a possible solution is reached. During the three stages various aids can be used to generate further ideas. These are called excursions and make use of word associations or images. In word associations, a word in the client's 'how to' is used to spark off a succession of other words leading to absurd ideas or solutions. Images are described by participants who are encouraged to fantasise and build on previous fantasies. Absurd solutions may be reached and these are taken by the group and made to fit (known as 'force-fit') the reality of the client's problem. While the images or fantasies may be completely wild and bear no relation to the problem, an effort is always made to relate, i.e. force-fit, them to the reality of the client's problem.

Possible solution and next steps

This is the final stage of the process where the client commits himself to the possible solution by stating what he likes about it, what is new and what is feasible. He also states the next steps he will take to implement the solution, thus committing himself publicly to act.

Ideally, a synectics session lasts not more than 40 minutes, and a possible solution has been produced which the client likes and is committed to by his statement of the next steps. A potential snag lies in the choice by the client of the ideas to be investigated, particularly by his comments in the itemised response — the client may miss another and potentially more rewarding avenue to be explored. The participants may see it and be frustrated by the client's reluctance or obtuseness in taking another idea.

In comparison with brainstorming, synectics has some major differences. In synectics the creative or divergent stages are relatively short and are interspersed with analytical or convergent stages. Participants may find it difficult to switch from one to the other. The leader does not take part in the content of the session; he is merely a recorder of the ideas and controller of the process. This can be frustrating, particularly where the leader himself has ideas to contribute. The client may miss an easy and obvious way in his itemised response. Participants may see other less obvious solutions which should be investigated, but the process does not allow this. Selection by the client commits him to possible solution — if the participants select it, the client would be uncommitted.

While these comments may appear to show synectics in a less favourable light than brainstorming, the synectics process does have the advantage of leading to possible solutions in a very short time — about 40 minutes. Brainstorming with its much longer creative or divergent stage and the time-consuming evaluation process, will not produce the useful ideas in such a short time. Brainstorming, however, does have an advantage in producing a much larger number of ideas, which can be examined.

Attribute listing

This creative technique is applicable more to tangible objects than to ideas. The attributes or characteristics of an object are identified and recorded. Each attribute is then separately examined to see whether it can be improved or changed.

An example of the application of attribute listing is to think of improvements to that most common do-it-yourself instrument, the screwdriver. The attributes of a screwdriver can be listed as follows:

metal, preferably steel, shank

shank is round

flat wedge end to fit the head of the screw

shank fixed into a wooden handle in line with the shank

manually operated

twisted to get torque

handle must be released and regripped after each twist

handle shaped for gripping by the hand

This list of attributes — and there are more — is questioned in considerable detail to see whether changes could be made. This leads to fundamental improvements in the operation of the screw-driver, bearing in mind its purpose — to fix something to something else by means of a threaded piece of metal, a screw. For example:

The flat wedge end could be changed to a cruciform shape.

The handle could be made to incorporate several different shanks to fit different types of screws.

A ratchet could be fitted to avoid the need for releasing and regripping the shank.

The handle could be adapted to a pistol grip rather than the straight grip.

The handle could be made to incorporate other tools or possibly different sized shanks.

The materials of the shank and handle could be improved or cheapened.

The method of fixing the shank to the handle could be changed or simplified.

A spanner flat could be corporated in the steel shank.

Several of these changes are now seen in screwdrivers, particularly those designed for special applications.

Another use of attribute listing is to take an attribute and see whether it could be applied in a completely different field. The spread of rental activities is said to have started in car rental, which was seen to be profitable, and is now to be found in many quite different fields such as TV rental, tool and equipment renting, clothes renting, rent-a-crowd and many others.

Forced relationships

This technique takes objects or ideas and asks the question: 'If these were combined, what new object or idea would be produced?' Two or more quite unrelated products can be combined to give a totally new product.

As an example, the manufacturer of furniture could take two of the items he produces and see whether they could be combined to make a new or saleable item. The type of chair seen in some training schools which incorporates a writing surface could have been designed by combining the conventional arm chair and the table. Consciously or unconsciously, this technique is being used to a considerable extent with the advent of miniaturisation and micro-processors. The digital wrist watch which combines a stop-watch, calendar and a calculator is just such an example. Ballpoint pens which include a watch or a cigarette lighter are further examples. An example from bygone days is the pen or pencil which contained up to four different coloured ballpoint pens or coloured leads. Returning to the furniture industry, there is on the market an electrically heated trouser press which incorporates a shelf on top for small change or the contents of pockets, a pull out rod on which ties can be hung and a hanger at the back to take a shirt or a jacket.

Morphological analysis

This technique is similar to attribute listing. It takes all the possible variables to a problem and seeks to combine them in new ways. Some of these new ways may exist, or be quite impossible, but others may be novel, and worth developing.

An example is the development of a new form of transport. The variables could be analysed:

Travelling in   : air, water, space, underground.

Travelling on   : wheels, rollers, air cushion, skids, magnetic cushion.

Powered by   : steam, gas, cable, atomic, electricity, energy stored in flywheels.

Traveller   : sitting, lying, standing, hanging.

The combination of $4 \times 5 \times 6 \times 4$ gives 480 different forms of tranpsort, many of which exist. For example, air + skids + cable + standing gives a ski lift. Underground + wheels + electricity + standing gives London Transport in the rush hour!

A modification is to list the variables on strips of paper under the main heading. The strips are placed alongside each other, and moved to give new combinations. Alternatively, the variables can be listed on coloured cards and shuffled to give different combinations.

Lateral thinking and PO

(With acknowledgement to Dr Edward de Bono.)
Analytical thinking, as we have seen, is a logical thought

process usually involving judgement and analysis, and with only two possible outcomes. These are acceptance or rejection of an idea, i.e. yes or no. All too often, and particularly with new, strange or untried ideas, rejection (or no) is the outcome.

Creative thinking is a wide-ranging or lateral process requiring suspended judgement, and a willingness to bring out all ideas however silly or wild. As we have seen, this is difficult for the analytically trained manager. A device to delay judgement is to preface the idea with the word 'PO'. This says in effect, 'Give the idea a chance, don't kill it too quickly, because it may lead to useful ideas'. The wildest idea technique in brainstorming is similar in that useful ideas may be developed from the silliest idea.

PO can be used as a way out of a difficult or impossible situation. If a line of argument leads to a dead end or a block, the use of PO may show a way round the block. Prefacing subsequent ideas or suggestions with PO acknowledges that they may be silly. Deferring judgement on the idea may however lead to other ideas, not so silly, and eventually to useful ideas.

The concept of PO is developed in de Bono's book *Lateral Thinking, a Textbook of Creativity* (see Bibliography).

Check lists

This technique builds lists to stimulate ideas, or to prevent them being forgotten. One well-known check list is Osborn's generalised check list, developed by Alex F. Osborn (see Bibliography). In this list, the main headings are:

Put to other uses?

Adapt?

Modify?

Magnify?

Minify?

Substitute?

Rearrange?

Reverse?

Combine?

This check list can be used to question ideas or objects, and can result in new ideas being developed. An advertising campaign for a fizzy drink can be supported by a bottle opener five times larger than normal (i.e. magnify?) with slogans or recipes for drinks painted on it. 'Put to other uses?' is the basis of the warm-up session mentioned in Chapter 2 on brainstorming.

Bibliography

There are relatively few books on creative thinking as applied to management, and fewer on the methodology of brainstorming. The list below gives a selection of authors, and one title for each author, all of whom have provided useful background material for the talks and seminars given by the author. Some authors have written many books, and their other titles will be found in their book quoted below.

From time to time articles have appeared in publications and papers. A selection of these is included.

Books

Adams, James L., *Conceptual Blockbusting, A Guide to Better Ideas,* San Francisco (1974), W.H. Freeman and Company.

Buzan, Tony, *Use Your Head*, BBC Publications (1974).

de Bono, Edward, *Lateral Thinking, A Textbook of Creativity*, Ward Lock. Just one of a number of useful books by Edward de Bono.

Dudeney, H.E., *Puzzles and Curious Problems*, Fontana. Another series of puzzle books.
Emmet, E.R., *A Diversity of Puzzles*, New York (1972). Barnes and Noble Books, a division of Harper and Row.

Gardner, Martin, *Mathematical Puzzles and Diversions*, Pelican A713. One of a number of books on puzzles which are amenable to both creative and analytical treatments.

Gordon, William J.J., *Synectics*, New York (1961), Harper and Row.

Jackson, K.F., *The Art of Solving Problems*, Heinemann (1975). A useful book covering all stages of problem solving. Creative thinking and brainstorming are discussed, but unfortunately the 'wrong' method of introducing brainstorming to newcomers is given on p. 124 — see p. 86 in Chapter 5 of this book.

Koestler, Arthur, *The Act of Creation*, Hutchinson (1964), Pan Piper (1970) and Pan Picador (1975). The best book on creativity with links to art and humour, and a reference for 'bisociative thinking'.

Lanners, Edi (ed.), *Illusions*, Thames and Hudson (1977).

Mott, Jacolyn A., *Creativity and Imagination*, Mankato, USA (1973), Creative Education Inc.

Osborn, Alex F., *Applied Imagination*, New York (1957), Charles Scribner and Sons. The original book by the founding father of brainstorming.

Parnes, S.J., and Harding, H.F., *A Source Book for Creative Problem Solving*, Charles Scribner and Sons (1962). One of a series of books from the one-time director (S.J. Parnes) of the Creative Education

Foundation.

Prince, G.M., *The Practice of Creativity*, New York (1970), Harper.

Rickards, Tudor, *Problem Solving Through Creative Analysis*, Gower Press (1974). A useful book by the founder of the creativity programmes at the Manchester Business School.

Simberg, A.L., *Creativity at Work*, Industrial Education Institute (1964).

Smith, J. Nickle, *Understanding Creativity, A Lightning Course for Executives*, Rugby (1973), Mantec Publications. A fun book with much sound creative sense.

Taylor, Irving A., and Getzels, J.W. (eds), *Perspectives in Creativity*, Chicago, Aldine Publishing Company.

Walter, W. Grey, *The Living Brain*, Gerald Duckworth (1973) and Pelican (1961).

Whiting, Charles S., *Creative Thinking*, Chapman and Hall (1958).

Papers and articles

'Creative thinking and brainstorming', British Institute of Management Foundation, 1980.

'You and creativity', *Kaiser Aluminium News,* vol. 25, no. 3.

'The nature of creativity', J.J. Field, *Advertising Quarterly,* no. 17, Autumn 1968.

'Creativity and design', P.R. Whitfield, *Chartered Mechanical Engineer,* January 1969.

'The three domains of creativity', Arthur Koestler, *British Mensa Journal*, 108, February 1968.

'Creative thinking package', *Industrial Training International*, vol. 2, no. 2, February 1972. Gives an evaluation of the tape/slide training programme mentioned below.

'Procedures for managers in idea deficient situations: an examination of brainstorming approaches', T. Rickards and B.L. Freedman, *Journal of Management Studies*, vol. 15, no. 1, February 1978.

Publications

Creativity in Action, a monthly publication by Sidney X. Shore, P.O. Box 603, Sharon, Connecticut 06069 USA.

Creativity Network, a quarterly publication edited by Tudor Rickards of the Manchester Business School.

Two other periodicals, *New Scientist* in the UK and *Scientific American* in the USA often have useful articles with a creativity angle.

Training packages

'Creative Thinking and Brainstorming', a tape/slide training programme featuring J.G. Rawlinson and produced by Management Training Ltd. Now marketed by Guild Sound and Vision Ltd, Peterborough. A very useful training package with a good leader's guide, 72 slides and a sound tape, covering the barriers to creative thinking and demonstrating brainstorming.

Glossary of Terms

Aha! The reaction to finding a solution. Also known as Eureka or the flash of illumination.

Analytical thinking A logical thought process leading to one or a small number of solutions.

Attribute listing One of the lesser known creativity techniques, used mainly on tangible problems. The attributes or characteristics of the problem or object are identified and examined in turn, with the objective of finding improvements.

Barriers Things that get in the way of, or prevent, creativity and which need to be removed before using creative techniques.

Bisociative thinking The term coined by Arthur Koestler to show the linking of two unrelated planes or matrices in the creative act. Also used in the analysis of humour and the joke.

Brainstorming The best known of the creative techniques, and defined as 'a means of getting a large number of ideas from a group of people in a short time'. The technique was developed by Alex F. Osborn in the 1930s.

Challenging the obvious One of the barriers to creative thinking. We accept the obvious and do not challenge it enough.

Check list   A list to stimulate new ideas or to prevent ideas being forgotten. Osborn's generalised check list is one of the more stimulating.

Conformity   One of the barriers to creative thinking, and sometimes described as 'giving the answer expected'.

Convergent   The term for analytical thinking, where the process converges to a single answer (cf. divergent).

Creative thinking   Defined as 'the relating of things or ideas which were previously unrelated' (cf. bisociative thinking).

Cross-fertilise   One of the four guidelines in brainstorming, meaning to pick up and develop ideas of others in the group.

Devil's advocate   A technique which deliberately takes the contrary view to find fault (cf. reverse brainstorming).

Divergent   The term for creative thinking where the process diverges to a large number of ideas and ranges far and wide over the problem (cf. convergent).

Drying-up   A stage in brainstorming where the flow of ideas falls away or dries up completely. Several techniques are available to re-stimulate the flow of ideas (cf. incubation).

Effort   One of the stages in thinking, and can lead to frustration when ideas are 'on the tip of my tongue' and cannot be reached.

Eureka   'I have found it' — the happy exclamation on solving a problem (e.g. Aha!)

Evaluating too quickly   One of the barriers to creative thinking, where the well-developed analytical ability rejects an idea with the phrase 'That's silly, that won't work'.

Evaluation The final stage in brainstorming, where the large number of ideas are refined to the few ideas which can be implemented.

Fear of looking a fool The biggest of the barriers to creative thinking.

Forced relationship A creative technique in which two or more objects are combined to make a new object.

Freewheel One of the four guidelines, meaning to dream, or let go of inhibitions.

How to ... The words prefacing a restatement — the key being to make sense in a literal way of the restatement, including the words 'How to ...'.

'In how many ways can we ...' The words prefacing the selected restatements for a brainstorming session.

Incubation The method in brainstorming for stimulating further ideas by reading silently the lists of ideas.

Insight The flash of illumination on a problem, when a solution is seen (cf. Aha! and Eureka).

Lateral thinking A term for creative thinking where the mind ranges far and wide in seeking ideas (e.g. divergent).

Morphological analysis A creative technique which identifies all variables in a problem, and combines them in different ways.

One unique answer One of the barriers to creative thinking where the analytical man seeks a pattern giving just one answer.

Quantity One of the four guidelines, urging a

brainstorming group to find large numbers of ideas, without worrying about quality.

Repeat technique   The method of identifying repeated ideas with an objective of generating further ideas.

Restating the problem   The first stage in brainstorming when the problem is examined from different viewpoints by asking the question 'How to . . .'. Also a problem-solving technique in its own right.

Reverse brainstorming   A creative technique used after evaluation and asking the question 'In how many ways can this idea fail?' Sometimes known as 'devil's advocate'.

Self-imposed barrier   One of the barriers to creative thinking, where the barriers are put up by oneself and may not exist at all.

Suspend judgement   The most important of the four guidelines. No evaluation is allowed in a brainstorming session and judgement is put on one side.

Synectics   A creative technique similar to brain-storming.

Vertical thinking   A term for analytical thinking, where deep narrow probing of the facts is used to identify solutions (e.g. convergent).

Warm-up session   A stage in brainstorming to make a group free-wheel and laugh.

Wildest idea   A creative technique which takes the wildest and silliest idea from a brain-storming session and seeks to turn it into a good idea.

INDEX

This index includes topics and names. The references are shown, e.g. 3/27, the first figure being the chapter, and the second the page number in the book.